Tune-Up & Electrical Service

A mini-course for the do-it-yourselfer
who wants to learn how to do it right.

Do-It-Right Publishing, Inc.
Van Nuys, California

Published and distributed by

Do-It-Right Publishing, Inc.
Post Office Box 839
Newhall, CA 91322-0839

Written by: Michael Bishop
                   Dennis Holmes

Series Concept
& Design by: Dennis Holmes

Production by: Steve Janowski

Photography by: Patrick Holmes

Illustration by: Steve Amos

FIRST EDITION
First printing, 1991
Second printing, 1991
Third printing, 1992
Fourth printing, 1993

Library of Congress Card Number: 90-84028

ISBN 1-879110-15-6

Proudly printed in the United States of America.

10 9 8 7 6 5

FOREWORD

This book covers two major areas of DIY work: tune-up and electrical service. Doing these jobs yourself saves you a substantial amount of money—the prime motivation for DIY work! In addition, a good tune-up gives you (1) maximum power and gas mileage from your engine and (2) minimum exhaust emissions for cleaner air.

A major goal of this book is to teach you a broad understanding of tune-up and electrical service work. We do this by showing you the techniques, short-cuts, and quality tips that are used by factory-trained professional technicians. Whether you are a beginner or a moderately experienced do-it-yourselfer, we want you to look over the shoulder of a pro and learn more about *what* he does—and *why*.

The organization of the *Tune Up* section is important: it takes you through the thinking process of a professional as he would perform a tune up on virtually any gasoline engine—from an assessment of basic mechanical soundness to the precise setting of ignition and fuel system adjustments. Too often, the amateur mechanic views a tune-up as simply replacing the plugs and tweaking a few adjustments. The professional approach is far more searching—inspecting and testing every component that ultimately delivers fuel and ignition to the combustion chamber. And replacing those found faulty.

Got a modern fuel-injected engine with sophisticated computer-controlled ignition? Too many DIYer's think there's nothing left for them to do, so they do *nothing!* Big mistake. These engines have even more critical needs for frequent fuel and air filter replacement and for inspection (and possible replacement) of ignition cables. We give you a complete run-down of what you should check and why.

The *Electrical Service* section covers the really important jobs that DIYers most commonly do. And these jobs are pretty much the same, whether you're driving a new car or one that's 25 years old. Here, we give you a lot of information about battery service, electrical component replacement, and troubleshooting. These jobs are big money-savers for DIYers.

In reading this book, let your mind be tuned-in to getting the *big picture.* What you learn now will help you with the car or truck your working on today—and with all the vehicles you work on in the future.

As compared to a shop manual, think of this as a *job-specific* book, with application to a broad number of engines and systems. We've tried to take you inside the mind of a professional technician—to show you what he looks at and how he does each job. We show you the most common mistakes and how to avoid them. We tell you which jobs have a good payoff for the DIYer and which jobs you should steer clear of.

In short, this is a mini-course on tune-up and electrical service for the DIYer! We hope it builds your skill, improves the quality and speed of your work, and saves you some big money.

THANKS

Thanks to our partners—Steve McKee, Lonetta Holmes, and John Dawson—for their enthusiastic encouragement and go-for-it attitude in helping launch this new series. Without them, these books would not be.

Thanks to Vance Lausmann for his technical review and important suggestions. He is the mechanic's mechanic.

Thanks to Bert Poncher for freely sharing his 25 years of experience in the auto aftermarket industry with us "kids."

Thanks to Dan Hackett and Karl Anthony for technical assistance in electronic page production. Thanks to Jana Brett for assistance in cover design.

Thanks to Nissan Motor Corporation in U.S.A. and Hyundai Motor America for their support and endorsement of our model-specific manual series. They have helped us prove the validity of our communication concepts, and they have made a lot of their customers quite happy in the process.

And thanks to the 35,000+ professional technicians in Toyota, Nissan, Honda, and Hyundai dealerships for whom we have developed factory training programs and manuals over the past 17 years. It was *you* who taught, and we who learned.

THE SPECIFICATIONS YOU NEED

The best place to find the most accurate specs for a proper tune-up is right under the hood! The Emissions Label lists idle speed, ignition advance, and—as needed for older vehicles—fast idle speed, mixture, etc. Factory-trained technicians are taught that this is the *best* source for accurate tune-up specifications.

Underhood Emissions Label

PROFESSIONAL TIPS AND TECHNIQUES FOR

TUNE-UP & ELECTRICAL SERVICE

- FOR ALL ENGINES: Total tune-up saves big $$$.
- How to inspect & replace spark plugs, ignition wires, air & fuel filters, alternator & starter.
- Carburetor cleaning & performance tuning.
- Battery, headlight & electrical troubleshooting.
- Avoid expensive mistakes—Hundreds of photos show you the Do-It-Right way.

= What you need to know!

The Emissions Label plus this Do-It-Right book
equals what you need to know for a tune-up.

The nice thing is that you can be sure that the specifications on the underhood label are precisely right for *your engine.* They take into account mid-year changes and special equipment on your vehicle.

Contents At-a-Glance

Detailed Contents

IMPORTANT SAFETY NOTICE

Pay special heed to the *warnings* in this book. They are intended to help protect you and your vehicle. When lifting your vehicle, make sure it is securely supported on jackstands before performing any work underneath it. Do *not* rely on the jack that came with your car or truck for safe support.

You should use standard and accepted safety precautions and equipment when handling toxic or flammable fluids. You should wear safety goggles or other protection during cutting, grinding, chiseling, prying, or any other similar process that can cause material removal or projectiles.

Following proper service procedures is essential for your safety and the correct functioning of your vehicle. We believe that the general service procedures in this book are described in such a manner that they may be performed safely and properly on a wide variety of vehicles. However, it is your responsibility to determine the precise applicability of these procedures to your specific vehicle or engine.

Please note that the condition of your vehicle, or the level of your mechanical skill, or your level of reading comprehension may result in or contribute in some way to an occurrence which causes injury to yourself or damage to your vehicle. It is not possible to anticipate all of the conceivable ways or conditions under which cars and trucks may be serviced, or to provide warnings as to all of the possible hazards that may result. Accordingly, because of these conditions which are unknown to us and are beyond our control, our liability must be and is limited to the cost of this book.

If you use service procedures, tools, or parts which are not specifically recommended in this book you must first completely satisfy yourself that neither your safety nor the safety of your vehicle will be jeopardized. All liability is expressly disclaimed for any injury or damage if you fail in any respect to follow all of the instructions and warnings given in any procedure in this book.

Although the information in this book is based on industry sources and experts, it is possible that changes in designs may be made which could not be included here. While striving for precise accuracy, Do-It-Right Publishing, Inc. cannot assume responsibility for any errors, changes, or omissions that may occur in the information presented here.

Part A:
Tune-Up

SOME GOLDEN RULES OF CAR AND TRUCK MAINTENANCE

■ Perform routine maintenance more frequently than the manufacturer recommends. Spark plugs, filters, and lubricants are cheap. Engines are expensive.

■ Before you begin a job, read this book for an overview of the procedure and for important tips on doing it right. For each vehicle you work on, read the Owner's Manual and any shop manual you may have.

■ Before you begin, get together *all* the tools, supplies, and parts you will need. Don't get caught half-way through a job and then discover you need to drive back to the store with the car you're working on!

■ Work safely. Think about your own safety and the safety of your vehicle. Read the Safety Notice in the front of this book. Use common sense.

Section 1:

Tune-Up Overview

WHAT'S REQUIRED FOR A QUALITY TUNE-UP?

A quality tune-up requires that you pay careful attention to those factors that are essential for the correct operation of your engine. To tune up any engine, you must always check the following items:

- **Cylinder and valve condition**—The piston rings and valves must create a good seal in all of the cylinders. Good compression is essential for both power and economy from your engine.

- **Fuel/air supply and mixture**—A clean, unrestricted supply of air and fuel must be available, and delivered in the correct mixture ratio required by the engine at any given time.

■ **Spark intensity and timing**—An intense spark must be provided at the precise instant it's needed to ignite the fuel/air mixture in the cylinder.

Many of the items that affect these systems can be serviced by a do-it-yourselfer with very simple tools. That's the focus of this book. Over a period of a year, you can save a nice bit of money, plus learn a great deal about how your engine works!

This 1990 high-tech fuel-injected engine needs regular "tune-up" maintenance. It has electronic ignition with 6 integrated coil units and no distributor. A computer "black box" totally controls the FI unit. Yet it still needs regular replacement of air and fuel filters and a total checkout of cables and connectors.

This 1968 Chevy engine needs regular "tune-up" adjustments and maintenance. It has a carburetor with several adjustment screws, a mechanical distributor, and no "black boxes." Yet it, too, needs regular replacement of the air and fuel filters and a total checkout of cables and connectors to ensure proper operation.

THE CORRECT STEPS AND SEQUENCE FOR A TUNE-UP

A good tune-up consists of five basic "steps" of inspection, adjustment, and replacement. Each step can affect the steps that follow. It is important that you do each step in this specific order:

1. **Mechanical valves only: check and adjust clearance.** Correct valve clearance is required for correct valve-to-seat sealing and is necessary before performing a . . .

2. **Compression test.** This tells you a lot about the health of your engine and lets you know what to expect in future repair work. A compression test also lets you know that you won't be wasting money by moving on to . . .

3. **Spark plug replacement.** The color and condition of the old spark plugs will help you with other steps in the tune-up. Plus, you're then ready to move on to . . .

4. **Ignition work.** Here, you check all ignition wiring and components, and adjust the timing. On older distributors, you also fine-tune the point gap and dwell. With the fire-starting equipment all working like it should, you're ready for...

5. **Carburetor or fuel injection work.** On modern carburetors and some fuel injection systems, the only adjustment you can make is idle speed. However, it is critical that you replace the air filter and fuel filter(s) regularly. If it's needed, you can also clean the carburetor and throttle linkage.

TUNING A MODERN "ELECTRONIC" ENGINE

Because we have produced official factory technician training programs and shop manuals for many years, we are quite aware of the needs of modern electronically controlled fuel-injected engines. If you have such an engine and it is running well, your "tune-up" workload will be quite a bit reduced—but not eliminated!

Many owners look under their hood, throw up their hands, and say "I can't work on this one, there's nothing for me to do!" Well, thankfully, there *are* fewer adjustments to get "out of spec" and cause your engine to run poorly. Most modern electronic fuel-injection systems *continuously adjust* the fuel flow and ignition timing for variations in coolant temperature, air density (altitude and temperature combined), engine load, and throttle setting. And the system may make these adjustments 30 times a second!

If your fuel-injected engine is running well, it generally means "there's nothing wrong with any of the black boxes." Just proceed with the normal maintenance-type tune-up shown in this book.

Even on the newest engines, you can still generally count on performing the following tune-up tasks:

■ **Compression check**—Compression has nothing to do with black boxes or fuel injection. But a compression check is vital for telling you about the overall *mechanical* condition of your engine.

■ **Spark plug replacement**—Still one of the most critical tasks in a tune-up. And since so many modern engines have aluminum heads, you must be particularly careful to do the job right, as we show you in this book.

■ **New air filter**—This is even *more important* on a lean-running modern emission-controlled engine than on older carbureted engines. Most modern fuel-injected systems have mixture determined by a "mass air sensor." What this means is that a clogged air filter may not cause a rough-running engine, but it sure will cost you top-end performance. You don't need to be an electronics wizard to put in a new air filter. Yet such a simple task can dramatically improve the performance of your fuel-injected engine!

■ **New fuel filter**—A fuel injector has a tiny hole that squirts a fine mist of gasoline. Even a microscopic bit of dirt can clog it. This means that fuel filter replacement on fuel injected engines is one of the most important jobs a do-it-yourselfer can do. (Sometimes, the fuel system will include more than one fuel filter.) This book gives you important instructions on relieving the internal pressure of fuel-injection systems before replacing the filter(s).

■ **Check timing and idle speed**—Most modern designs have made these nonadjustable. But every do-it-yourselfer should check to determine the exact requirements of each engine in the family. How? We show you how to read the under-hood emissions label to determine what is needed.

■ **Inspect and replace ignition wires—**
Modern ignition systems carry extremely high voltage, and wire condition is critically important to proper engine operation. Unfortunately, many modern engines often run with higher under-hood temperatures than those in the past, causing faster deterioration of the wiring. This is an easy inspection to make, and replacement by the do-it-yourselfer can save a substantial amount of money.

■ **Inspect all electrical and vacuum connectors—**Because computer-controlled engines rely so totally on sensor inputs from a number of sources, it is important that your tune-up include a thorough inspection of all under-hood wires and hoses. Even one loose fitting can send bad signals to the computer and cause problems.

What can't you do? If your modern high-tech engine is running poorly after completing these important tune-up tasks, you need to take it to a specialist—a technician with special test equipment and the training to use it. But be sure to tell him what you've already done, because *these are the items he too will check first!* Only when he has confirmed that the obvious things like compression, filters, and cables are okay will he proceed with deeper (and more complex) diagnosis.

A NOTE ON USING THIS BOOK

How you use this book—especially the first time—will depend a great deal on the first tune-up job you're going to tackle. But since the book is designed to build your overall skill and understanding of the tune-up process, we recommend you read the entire tune-up procedure given in Sections 2 through 7.

If You Have an Older Engine

This book covers all of the traditional tasks of a full tune-up. We show you how to adjust mechanical valves and how to (maybe) fix sticking hydraulic lifters. We show you how to use a spray cleaner to clean your carburetor without removing it from the engine, and we show you how to adjust mixture and fast idle speed on the oldie-but-goodie motors. If you have a mechanical distributor, we show you how to adjust timing, replace the points, set dwell, replace the rotor, and replace the distributor cap. (The authors own several '60's muscle cars, and we want you to keep your oldies going forever and running well!)

If You Have a Newer Engine

So far as tune-up work goes, you have fewer adjustments to make. Your focus will be on inspection and replacement. You can ignore such procedures as mechanical valve adjustment, distributor point and condenser replacement, and, in many cases, even timing and idle speed adjustment. Nonetheless, the book still gives you detailed instruction on every tune-up procedure that is within the skill and tool capability of the average do-it-yourselfer. And of course, the second half of this book, *Electrical Service,* is equally applicable to all vehicles—old or new!

CONSIDER ALL MAINTENANCE REQUIREMENTS

A final point: no matter what type of engine you have, do not forget that "tune-up" is only *half* the work your car or truck needs. The other important opportunity for do-it-your-selfers to save money is lubrication, oil-change, tranny service, shock replacement, and chassis maintenance. A companion book in this Professional Tips and Techniques series, *Lube, Oil, and Chassis Service,* may be helpful to you.

Section 2:

Tune-Up Parts, Supplies, and Tools

The "shopping list" shown on the following pages will help you get all of the things you need before you begin work.

When buying tools, parts, and supplies, it's smart to go with "name" brands. Products that have been around for a long time are generally very competitive. They offer good quality, suitability, and reasonable price. If they didn't, they wouldn't survive.

You may already own many of the tools you'll need to do the jobs in this book. But if you don't, we recommend that you buy only those you'll need for the jobs you plan to do. Buy quality rather than quantity. A good tool can last a lifetime.

Spark plugs—Normally, you should replace these at every tune-up (except for the platinum-tipped types). Make sure the type and heat range are right for your engine and driving conditions.

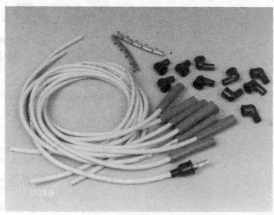

Ignition wires—These often break down internally and cause problems. Section 6 shows you how to inspect ignition wires and helps you decide which type to buy.

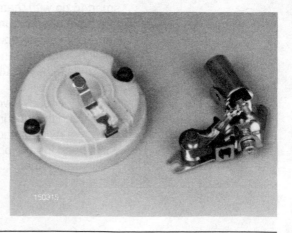

Points, condenser, rotor—If you have a non-electronic ignition, points and condenser are usually replaced at every tune-up.

Distributor cap—Section 6 shows you how to inspect and test the distributor cap. For your engine to run properly, it must not be cracked or worn.

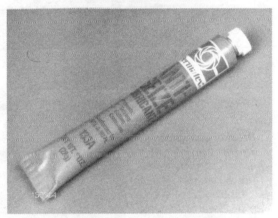

Anti-seize compound— This stuff is essential for installing spark plugs in modern engines with aluminum cylinder heads.

Carburetor cleaner—An important part of every tune-up on a carbureted engine is a thorough "wash down" of the carburetor. Section 7 shows you how to clean your carburetor in place.

Fuel injector cleaner—If your car is equipped with fuel injection, the injectors should be periodically treated to a dose of cleaner.

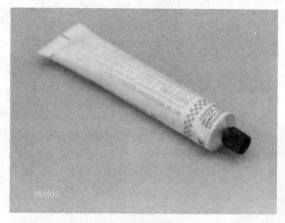

Breaker cam grease— Breaker cam lubrication prevents premature wear of the contact breaker rubbing block in conventional distributors.

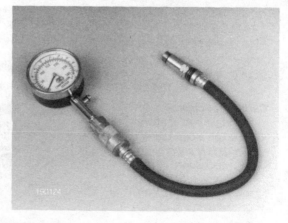

Compression gauge—A screw-in type is recommended, so you won't be dependent on a helper. Section 4 shows you how to perform a full compression test.

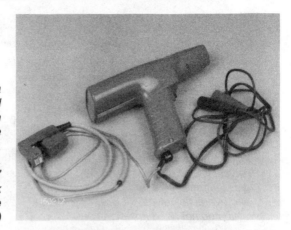

Timing light—Choose a bright battery-powered type, with an induction pickup. They're the easiest to use and read, even in bright sunlight. (Avoid cheap "neon" types; you have to work in a dark garage to see them.)

Volt/ohmmeter—Also called a multimeter or a VOM. This handy tool helps you evaluate the condition of ignition parts and assists in troubleshooting for electrical problems.

Spark plug wrench—The soft insert protects the porcelain insulation and holds the plug for you during removal and installation.

Flat feeler gauge—This is used for setting contact gap in conventional distributors and for adjusting mechanical valves. If your engine has electronic ignition and hydraulic valves, you do not need it.

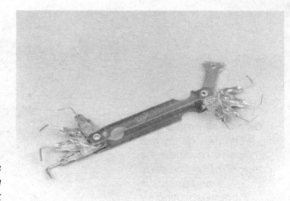

Ignition gauge—This is the best tool for checking and setting spark plug gap.

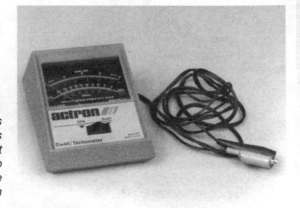

Dwell/tach—This two-function tool helps you check and adjust engine idle speed. It also allows you to fine-tune the contact breaker gap in conventional distributors.

Section 3:
Valve Adjustment

If your engine has *hydraulic* valve lifters (which is the vast majority of engines), they are automatically self adjusting. This section describes how they work and how to deal with them if they begin to "clatter." If your engine has *mechanical* lifters, you must check the valve clearances and, if necessary, adjust them as the first step in every routine tune-up.

If you are not sure whether your engine has hydraulic or mechanical lifters, check the maintenance schedule in your Owner's Manual. If it does *not* specify periodic valve inspection and adjustment, your engine has hydraulic lifters. If it *does* specify periodic valve adjustment, it has mechanical lifters, and you need to check and adjust them.

If valves with mechanical lifters are too loose, they will clatter, and fuel consumption and emissions may go up. Valves that are too tight will reduce performance and may "burn," causing expensive engine damage.

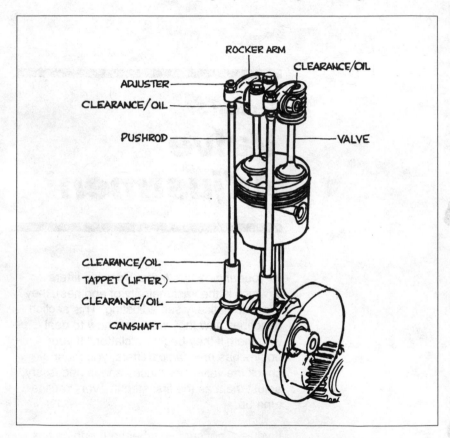

ROCKER ARM

CLEARANCE/OIL

ADJUSTER

CLEARANCE/OIL

PUSHROD

VALVE

CLEARANCE/OIL

TAPPET (LIFTER)

CLEARANCE/OIL

CAMSHAFT

Your engine's valve train was designed to operate with a small amount of clearance between the valves, rocker arms, and camshaft. *These clearances, measured in thousandths of an inch, are necessary to allow oil to lubricate the moving parts, and to allow the parts to expand as the engine warms up. Because parts wear, valve clearance will gradually change and require periodic adjustment.*

HOW MECHANICAL VALVE ADJUSTMENT WORKS

In most engines of a few decades ago—as well as a handful of imports today—valve adjustment is achieved in one of several ways:

1. With variable-length lock screws on the rocker arms that operate the valves.

2. With adjustable-length pushrods that fit between the lifters and the rocker arms.

3. With shims of different thicknesses placed between each lifter and the camshaft.

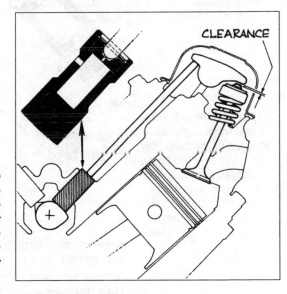

CLEARANCE

Typical solid lifter valve train. The lifter follows the cam lobe and moves the pushrod. This solid lifter is a fixed length. Valve clearance here is adjusted with a screw in the rocker arm.

In any of these arrangements, valve clearance adjustment is a compromise with more clearance at startup than at operating temperature. The result is valve clatter during warmup, and increasingly so as parts wear down between periodic adjustments. Today, almost all engines have hydraulic valve adjusters that don't require periodic adjustment.

HOW A HYDRAULIC VALVE LIFTER WORKS

A hydraulic valve lifter (or "adjuster" or "tappet") is a small piston-and-cylinder assembly, filled with engine oil, that takes up the excess clearance in a valve train. It can be installed between the cam and the pushrod, as shown below. Or in other engines, it can act directly on a rocker arm or a valve. If your engine does *not* require valve adjustment, you *do* have hydraulic lifters!

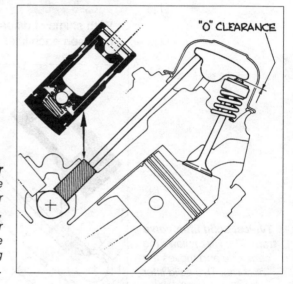

"O" CLEARANCE

Typical hydraulic-lifter valve train. *In the same location as the solid lifter on the preceding page, but this hydraulic lifter takes up excessive clearance by changing length.*

Small control ports in the lifter allow it to take in or get rid of oil to change length and compensate for changes in valve clearance. Thus, the hydraulic lifter maintains constant valve clearance despite different operating temperatures and normal wear in the valve train. The result is a quiet valve train that never needs adjusting or attention—*as long as the engine oil is changed regularly!* Because of their very tiny oil ports and passages, hydraulic lifters require clean engine oil. This is one big reason why you must change the engine oil and filter often.

WHAT TO DO ABOUT NOISY HYDRAULIC LIFTERS

When hydraulic lifters become clogged and sticky, the engine valve train makes a sharp clicking or clattering noise, particularly when cold. This usually occurs with just one lifter at first, but others will soon join in if the situation is not corrected. And don't be fooled because "the noise goes away when the engine warms up." Abnormal clicking is a warning that you better do something right away!

Besides the noise, sticking hydraulic lifters cause:

- Poor performance when a lifter fails to extend and fully open its valve.

- Poor performance plus *valve burning* when the lifter will not compress. In this case, the valve is not able to transfer heat to the cylinder head. The result? An expensive head overhaul!

At the first sign of sticking valve lifters, change the engine oil and filter. Then add a can of hydraulic lifter cleaning additive to the crankcase. There are several major brands in most auto parts departments, and they all work quite well. If the problem hasn't gotten so bad that there is damage, the lifters should quiet down within a few hundred miles.

If the noise persists, have it checked by your mechanic. If you let it go too long, you could be in for an expensive repair.

HOW TO ADJUST VALVES WITH SOLID LIFTERS

Before you can correctly adjust the valves, you must first warm up the engine until it reaches normal operating temperature (unless it's an air-cooled VW or Porsche, which are adjusted cold). Then shut it off, and remove the valve cover and distributor cap. Find the correct valve clearances in your Owner's Manual. Usually, the clearance for the exhaust valves will be greater than that for the intake valves.

In this job, you'll have to rotate the crankshaft several times to prepare each pair of valves for checking and adjustment. Always rotate the crankshaft clockwise, viewed from the crankshaft pulley. To make things easier, first remove all the spark plugs. (See *How to keep the spark plugs in order* on page 30.) To rotate the crankshaft, you need a 1/2-inch-drive socket wrench that fits the bolt on the end of the crankshaft. You will also need a breaker bar and possibly a short extension for the socket.

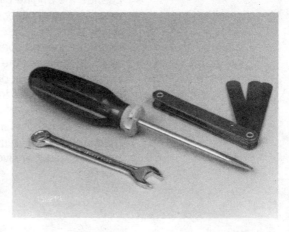

You'll need flat feeler gauges, a medium flat-blade screwdriver to turn the adjusters, and a box wrench that fits the adjuster locknut. This is usually a 1/2-inch wrench for domestic engines and 10-mm or 12-mm for most imports.

PRO TIP: When to Remove Spark Plugs from Aluminum Cylinder Heads

There are two times at which it's okay to remove spark plugs from aluminum cylinder heads:

1. When the engine has just been shut off, before it starts to cool down.

2. When it is completely cool.

When the engine is running, coolant in the head near the spark plugs keeps the plugs and the cylinder head at about the same temperature. However, when the engine is shut off and begins to cool down, the aluminum head cools—and shrinks—*faster* than the steel spark plugs. This causes the threads in the head to grip the spark plug threads, making the plugs difficult to remove. There is even a chance of the hard steel spark plug threads stripping the softer aluminum threads.

So, if you must adjust the valves in an aluminum cylinder head with the engine at operating temperature, remove the spark plugs as soon as the engine is shut off.

Coolant near the spark plug keeps the cylinder head and plug at about the same temperature when the engine is running.

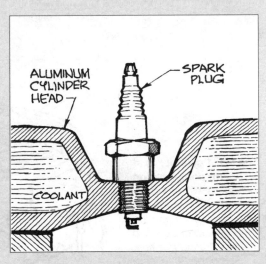

Begin by bringing the No. 1 cylinder to top-dead-center on compression. First identify your engine's No. 1 cylinder, using the illustration below. Then, with a wrench on the crankshaft, turn the engine over to bring the No. 1 piston to the top of its stroke with both valves closed.

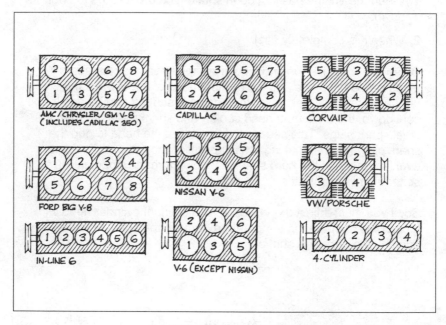

The No. 1 cylinder is at TDC on compression when the valve ends of both rocker arms are at their highest point and the distributor rotor points to the No. 1 firing position. *See page 28 to learn how to locate TDC.*

Check the clearance for the No. 1 intake valve. Slide the correct feeler gauge between the valve and adjuster. There should be a slight drag. Double check with the GO/NO-GO method: Insert the next smaller gauge. It should fit easily—GO. Then try the next larger gauge. It should not fit at all—NO-GO.

If adjustment is required, loosen the locknut. Hold the intake valve adjuster with a screwdriver and loosen the locknut with a box wrench.

Adjust the clearance. Slide the feeler gauge between the valve and the adjuster. Then, carefully turn the adjuster clockwise until there is a slight drag on the feeler gauge.

Tighten the locknut.
Hold the adjuster with the screwdriver to prevent it from turning, and tighten the locknut with the box wrench.

Recheck the clearance.
Make sure it didn't change when you tightened the locknut.

Check the clearance for the No. 1 exhaust valve.
Do this the same way you did for the intake valve. The clearance may be different so check your Owner's Manual. And remember to recheck the clearance after the locknut has been tightened.

When you have completed valve adjustment on cylinder No. 1, adjust the rest of the valves in the same way, in firing order. See Appendix A at the back of the book for the firing order for your engine.

Rotate the crankshaft to bring the next cylinder in the firing order to TDC on compression, and adjust both valves just as you did for cylinder No. 1.

4 Cylinder: Rotate the crankshaft 180° at a time.

In-line 6: Rotate the crankshaft 120° at a time.

V8: Rotate the crankshaft 90° at a time.

Continue to do this, one cylinder at a time, until all the valves are adjusted. Then, install the valve cover, and you're ready to move on to the compression toot.

PRO TIP: How to Find TDC Every Time

Your engine has a built-in, fool-proof indicator that tells you exactly when a cylinder is at TDC on compression. You'll find the indicator beneath the distributor cap. That's right—it's the distributor rotor.

When the No. 1 cylinder is at TDC on compression, the distributor rotor points to the position of the No. 1 spark plug wire terminal.

And, when the rotor points to the No. 2 spark plug terminal, cylinder No. 2 is at TDC on compression, and so on.

To prepare your distributor as an indicator, write the cylinder numbers on the distributor base directly below the corresponding spark plug wires. Begin at No. 1 and continue on, in firing order (see table in Appendix A).

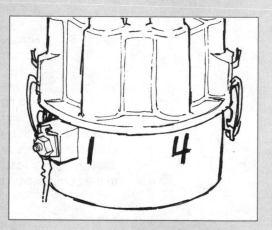

Next, remove the cap to uncover the rotor, and you have a TDC indicator that's pointing to the cylinder that's at TDC on compression— No. 1 in this case.

Section 4:
Compression Test

Often bypassed by do-it-yourselfers as "too much work," a compression test is important for determining the mechanical condition of your engine. (And it isn't much added work, since you will be replacing the spark plugs anyway.)

A compression test involves putting a gauge in each spark plug hole, turning over the engine, and measuring the pressure in each cylinder. The test shows you how well the piston rings and valves are sealing. Keeping a log of compression readings (Appendix B) will help you spot when an engine is wearing out and will need an overhaul. And if you have a troublesome "miss," a compression test can tell you whether it is caused by a burnt valve.

DRY AND WET TESTS

Compression should be checked first with the cylinders "dry." This means that they are tested just as they were last run, when the engine was shut off. Then if low compression is discovered in one or all cylinders, those with low readings should be retested "wet."

For a wet compression test, pour a teaspoon or so of oil into the cylinder through the spark plug hole. Crank the engine a few turns to distribute the oil, and then measure the compression again. If the compression comes up to normal this time, the cylinders or piston rings (or both) are worn and will no longer maintain good compression.

If the compression remains low, where it was during the dry test, this means that a valve is not sealing. It could be burned or warped, or the valve seat may be burned or eroded.

PRO TIP: How to Keep Spark Plugs in Order

Don't just line up the old spark plugs on a bench or the pavement, hoping that they'll stay in order.

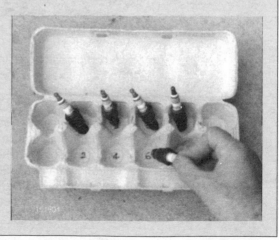

To know exactly which plug came from which cylinder for subsequent "reading" (page 38) use an old egg carton. Mark each compartment with the correct cylinder number. (Chart on page 24.)

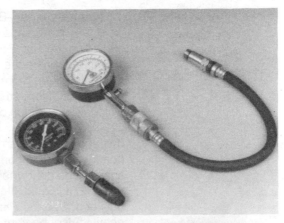

There are two types of compression gauges: push-in and screw-in. The screw-in type is easiest to use if you are working alone without a remote starter switch.

Do a "dry" test first. Screw (or hold) the gauge into the first cylinder, and crank the engine through 2-3 revolutions—until the gauge needle no longer rises. Then, record the reading on a sheet of paper. Do the same for all of the cylinders and check the Quick-Check Table, page 33, for diagnosis.

Do a "wet" test only if there's a problem. If one or more cylinders have very low compression—less than 75 percent of the highest cylinders—put a teaspoon (or several squirts from an oil can) of engine oil in the low cylinder, crank it several times to distribute the oil, and retest it.

HOW TO PERFORM A COMPRESSION TEST

1. Remove plugs—Before you start, remove all of the spark plugs. Keep them in order as shown on the *Pro Tip* on page 30. You'll be "reading" them in the next section to determine even more about your engine's current condition, so it's important you know which cylinder each plug came from.

If your engine has an aluminum cylinder head, it is very important that you remove the spark plugs only when (1) it is fully warmed up or (2) it is cold. No temperature in between. See the *Pro Tip* on page 23 for details. Also, be very careful not to cross-thread your spark plugs in an aluminum head.

2. Disable ignition—If your vehicle has a conventional breaker point ignition, disconnect the primary wire from the coil to prevent spark. If it has an electronic ignition, disconnect the plug to the control box. Do not disconnect the wire at the coil or ground the high-tension coil wire—you will damage the control box.

3. Open the throttle—This simply ensures that the engine will get enough air to give you an accurate reading. If you're working with an assistant, hold the throttle pedal down as you crank the engine with the ignition key. If you're working alone, you can put a heavy weight on the pedal.

4. Crank the engine and read compression of each cylinder—If you're working alone, hook up a remote starter switch as shown in the *Pro Tip* on page 34.

HOW TO INTERPRET COMPRESSION TEST RESULTS

The Quick-Check Table below indicates general cylinder condition for several compression ratios (8:1, 9:1, 10:1) along with acceptable cylinder-to-cylinder variations.

If one or more cylinders is substantially lower than the others during a dry compression test, wet test the low cylinders and compare the results to the dry test. If the compression has not increased, it's likely that the cylinder has a burnt or warped valve. This requires a valve job to correct the situation. (The problem could also be caused by a hole in the piston, but that's not as likely.)

If compression during the wet test comes up to or near the compression of the good cylinders, the problem is likely caused by a worn cylinder or rings. This requires re-ringing and possibly a rebore and new pistons to correct.

Quick-Check Table: Cylinder Condition

Condition	Cylinder Pressure, psi		
Compression Ratio	8:1	9:1	10:1
Normal compression reading	105-120	120-135	140-160
Minimum allowable, any cylinder	90	100	120
Max difference between cylinders	20	20	25

NOTE: Engines with high-performance camshafts will usually show 10-15 psi less than engines with standard camshafts.

PRO TIP: How to Connect a Remote Starter Switch

A remote starter switch is a big time saver for such jobs as compression testing and setting the dwell angle on distributor points.

Some cars and trucks are equipped with a remote solenoid or a junction block, usually mounted on the firewall or on the inner fender, on the starter side of the engine. On other vehicles, the solenoid and the connections are located on the starter. In either case, hookup of the remote starter switch is the same.

■ Connect one wire to the battery terminal on the solenoid.

■ Connect the other wire to the "S" terminal on the starter solenoid.

Be extremely careful not to ground the remote switch wires to any other part of the vehicle. Three typical connections are shown in the following illustrations.

Typical General Motors (and many others) remote starter hook up. One remote-starter wire is connected to the battery terminal on the solenoid; the other wire is connected to the "S" terminal.

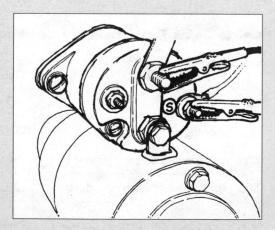

Typical Chrysler remote starter hook up. One wire to battery terminal on junction block. To attach the other wire from the remote switch, note how you slide back the starter wire, but leave it connected.

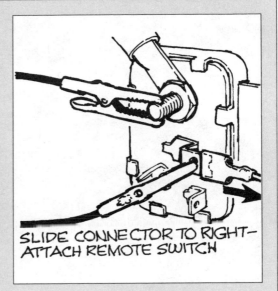

SLIDE CONNECTOR TO RIGHT-
ATTACH REMOTE SWITCH

Typical Ford remote starter hook up. Note how the starter wire is disconnected from the solenoid, and one wire from the remote switch is connected to the terminal. The other wire from the remote switch connects to the large battery cable terminal on the solenoid.

REMOVE WIRE
& ATTACH
REMOTE SWITCH

Section 5:

Spark Plugs

(as shown in the Pro Tip on page 30)

WHAT OLD PLUGS TELL YOU ABOUT YOUR ENGINE

Mention "tune-up" and what's the first thing that comes to mind? Spark plugs! Whether you're just cleaning and regapping your old plugs or installing new ones, these hard-working parts deserve more attention than they usually get. Even if a compression test indicates that your engine is in good condition, it's still important to "read" the old spark plugs for other conditions. Keep the plugs in order (as shown in the Pro Tip on page 30) so you will know which cylinders are affected by any problems you discover.

The conditions shown on the following pages are the most common ones. Changing plug heat range will correct a few of the problems. But most will require another cure.

Appearance—Insulator is light tan or light gray with few or no deposits.

- *Causes*: Correct operating conditions.

- *Correction*: None. Clean, regap, reuse or replace with plug of same type and heat range.

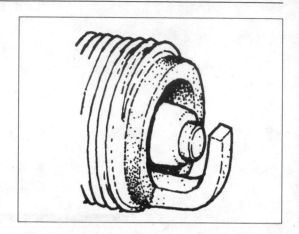

Appearance—Dull, dry black sooty carbon deposits on insulator, electrodes, and body.

- *Causes*: Mixture too rich, weak spark, choke not opening fully, dirty air cleaner, idling for long periods, heat range too cold.

- *Correction*: Clean, regap, and reuse after correcting problem; try hotter plug.

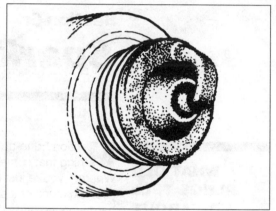

Appearance—Wet black deposits on insulator and plug body.

- *Causes*: Excess oil entering combustion chamber past worn rings, cylinder, or valve guides, or because of clogged PCV valve or hoses.

- *Correction*: Replace. Use a hotter plug if engine is not repaired.

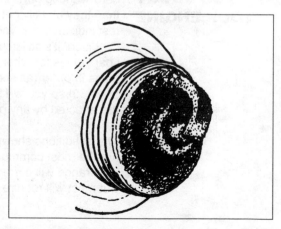

Appearance—Hard deposits (yellow, gray, black, or tan) on insulator.

■ *Causes*: Leaded gas, continuous low-speed driving resulting in dirty combustion chambers, heat range too hot.

■ *Correction*: Replace. "Exercise" engine on open road to clean combustion chambers; try colder plug.

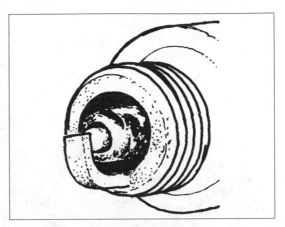

Appearance—Severely eroded electrodes.

■ *Causes*: Normal wear with lots of miles. However, if plugs are less than 6,000-miles old, they could be the wrong heat range (too hot). Also, incorrect coil polarity (see page 49) or some oil and fuel additives can cause this.

■ *Correction*: Replace.

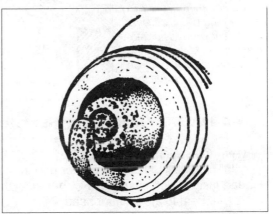

Appearance—Melted electrodes.

■ *Causes*: Too much ignition advance, inoperative advance, too-lean mixture, too-low octane fuel, carbon buildup in combustion chambers.

■ *Correction*: Replace. Check, correct timing, ignition advance mechanism, change fuel grade.

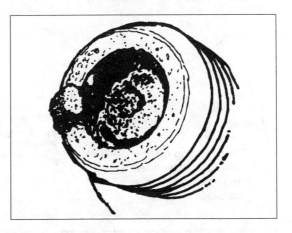

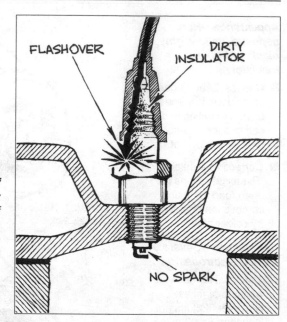

Inspect the outside of the spark plugs. *Greasy deposits on the outside of a plug can provide a spark path from the wire to the plug body, causing "flashover"—a hard-to-find misfire. Make sure the insulation is kept clean to prevent this.*

PRO TIP: What is Meant by Heat Range?

Heat range refers to a plug's ability to hold or get rid of heat. A "cold" plug has a shorter insulator and transfers heat to the cylinder head faster. "Hot" plugs have longer insulators and are slower to transfer heat to the cylinder head.

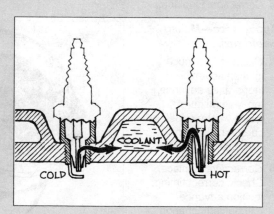

The cold plug on the left has a shorter heat transfer path *than the hot plug on the right.*

HOW TO KNOW IF YOU NEED HOTTER OR COLDER SPARK PLUGS

The spark plug specified for your engine is for "normal" driving. That's a combination of city and highway driving, in moderate weather and temperatures.

If most of your driving is stop-and-go in cool to cold weather, a *hotter* plug may work better. The higher temperature at the tip of the plug tends to burn off combustion deposits. This makes the plug self-cleaning.

If your old plugs have dull, dry black sooty carbon deposits like those shown in the middle illustration on page 38, they are probably too cold. Switch to a *hotter* plug.

If most of your driving is at highway speeds in hot weather, you may need a *colder* plug, which can withstand sustained high temperatures better than the normal type.

If your old plugs have hard deposits like those shown in the top illustration on page 39, they are probably too hot. Try switching to a *colder* plug.

Heat range coding is different for all major brands of spark plugs. Most stores that sell spark plugs have a chart to help you select the heat range you need for a number of brands.

HOW TO PREPARE AND INSTALL SPARK PLUGS

Whether you're reusing your old spark plugs after cleaning them or you're installing new spark plugs, they have to be correctly gapped for good performance. Some manufacturers put spark plug gap on the emissions label. Others put it in the Owner's Manual.

If your cylinder head is cast iron, apply a couple of drops of clean engine oil to the spark plug threads to make it easy to install the plugs now and to remove them at the next tune-up. But don't use oil with an aluminum head.

For an aluminum head, put anti-seize compound on the spark plug threads to make installation and removal easy and to reduce the risk of damaging the head. Be particularly careful threading spark plugs into an aluminum head. A cross-threaded spark plug can cut the threads out of an aluminum head—an expensive mistake. It can be done so easily, you may not realize what's happening until it's too late.

Usually, the head can be repaired. It's even possible to repair the head without removing it, but this isn't recommended. The best way is to remove the head, repair the threads, then reinstall the head. This little error can cost you about $300 to correct.

Another precaution for aluminum heads: Replace spark plugs only (1) when the engine is hot and has just been shut off or (2) when the engine is totally cold. Why? See the *Pro Tip* on page 23.

The following photos show you how to set the gap and install spark plugs.

Use a wire-type spark plug gauge to measure plug gap. *A flat feeler gauge gives false readings, particularly on old plugs where the side electrode is worn. The correct wire should "snap" through the gap with little force.*

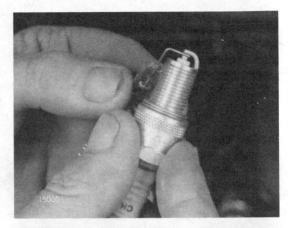

Adjust plug gap by bending the ground electrode. *Use the end of a gapping tool to carefully bend the side ground electrode either in or out near the base.*

For aluminum cylinder heads, apply anti-seize compound to all but the lower two or three threads of the spark plug. *Just a tiny dab is all you need, and keep it off of the insulation and electrodes, or it may short out the plug. For cast-iron heads, use a few drops of engine oil on the spark plug threads.*

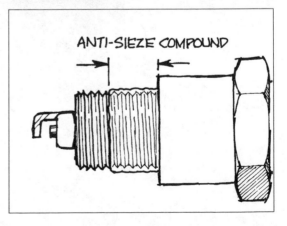

ANTI-SIEZE COMPOUND

Always screw spark plugs in by hand—never with a wrench. *This is very important for aluminum heads, where cross-threading can cause major damage. Hold the plug with the spark plug socket and an extension, and screw it in by hand until it contacts the seat. If the plug doesn't screw in easily, back it out and try again.*

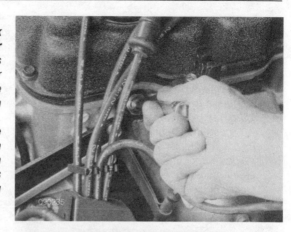

Tighten spark plugs carefully. *Once the plug is seated, tighten it with a wrench—1/4 turn if it has a gasket, or 1/8 turn if it's a taper-seat plug without a gasket. If you're really fussy, tighten the plugs to the torque recommended in your Owner's Manual— usually about 10-15 ft-lb for aluminum heads and 15-20 ft-lb for cast iron heads.*

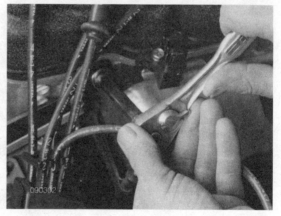

Section 6:
Distributor and Wires

This section includes some of the most important tasks in a tune-up: ignition wire testing, distributor inspection, and timing inspection and adjustment. If your engine is not getting the right spark at the right time, it simply can't run right!

In addition, if your engine has a distributor with points, this section shows you how to adjust gap and dwell, and how to replace the rotor, points, condenser, and distributor cap.

Give special attention to the inspections described here. Too many do-it-yourself mechanics give it a "once over lightly," yet visible damage and loose connections are often the cause of problems.

HOW TO TEST SPARK PLUG WIRES

Many times a rough-running engine will continue to run rough after hours of tune-up work, simply because bad spark plug wires were not replaced.

The problem seems to be that most folks don't realize that spark plug wires "wear out," just like other ignition parts. It takes only a few minutes to inspect and test the wires, so remember to include this essential step in your tune-up.

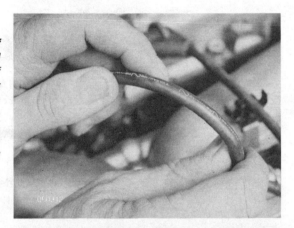

Check the condition of the insulation. It should be smooth and free of cracks and other damage. If the insulation is generally good, and the wires pass the resistance test in the next step, you can replace individual damaged wires. However, if the insulation is generally poor, replace the wires as a set.

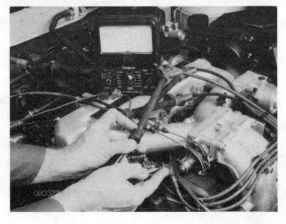

Measure the resistance of the wires. Disconnect the wires from the cap— one at a time. Touch a probe to each end of the wire. Compare the readings for all of the wires. They should all be within 10 percent of one another. If one or two are out of "spec," replace them. But, if readings vary widely, replace the entire set.

PRO TIP: Using an Analog Volt/ohmmeter

Analog meters must be zeroed each time they are used for a resistance test. To do this, set the meter to the R x 100 scale, turn the meter on, touch the probes together, and adjust the meter until the needle indicates 0 ohms.

To test the resistance of a spark plug wire, simply touch a meter probe to each end of the wire, and read the resistance on the R x 100 scale.

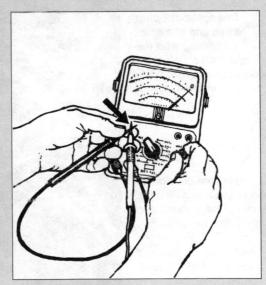

To zero the meter, select the R x 100 scale, touch the probes together, and adjust until the needle is at 0.

HOW TO REPLACE SPARK PLUG WIRES

New spark plug wires are available in preassembled sets, cut to length for your engine, and ready to install. (To select, cut, and prepare a "universal" set of wires for installation, see page 50.)

Change spark plug wires one at a time, beginning with the longest wire. *Select the longest wire from the new set, and match it up with the longest one on the engine.*

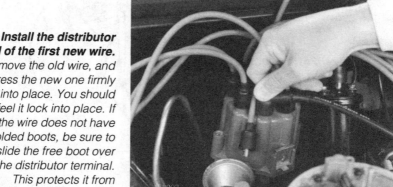

Install the distributor end of the first new wire. *Remove the old wire, and press the new one firmly into place. You should feel it lock into place. If the wire does not have molded boots, be sure to slide the free boot over the distributor terminal. This protects it from dirt and water.*

Install the spark plug end of the first new wire. Remove the old wire, and press the new one firmly onto the spark plug. Again, you should feel it lock into place. If your wire has a free boot, slide it firmly over the end of the spark plug.

Repeat the replacement process, one wire at a time. Replace the next-longest wire, then the next-longest, and so forth until the entire set is installed. By replacing wires one at a time, you ensure that you do not end up with a misfiring ignition, which could cause serious engine damage.

Double check the installation of your new wires to ensure they are connected correctly and there won't be any misfiring. Use the cylinder numbering chart on page 24 and the firing order listed for your engine in Appendix A.

HOW TO ASSEMBLE "UNIVERSAL" SPARK PLUG WIRES

Universal spark plug wire kits can save you a few dollars, and in some cases, may be your only choice. Make sure your kit has enough wires for your 4, 6, or 8-cylinder engine and that the terminals are the correct type. Usually, the wires have the distributor end assembled with the correct terminal and boot. You cut the wires to length, slide on the boot, and crimp on the spark plug terminal.

To avoid confusion, *replace just one wire at a time,* as shown on the preceding pages. Here's how to prepare a typical wire:

Use each old wire as a "pattern" to trim the new wire to the correct length. Start with the longest old wire, and trim the longest new one to the same length.

Slide a new distributor-end boot over the end of the trimmed wire. Expose several inches of wire below the boot. A quick spray of WD-40 makes it easier to slide the boot over the wire.

Strip 1/2 inch of insulation from the end of the wire. *Take care not to cut through the conductor core.*

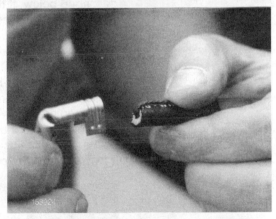

Fold the exposed conductor back over the insulation, *and slide the connector over the folded conductor.*

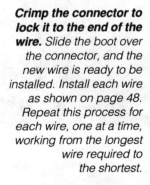

Crimp the connector to lock it to the end of the wire. *Slide the boot over the connector, and the new wire is ready to be installed. Install each wire as shown on page 48. Repeat this process for each wire, one at a time, working from the longest wire required to the shortest.*

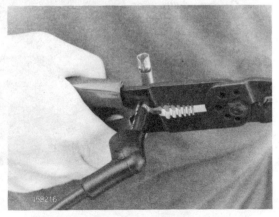

HOW TO INSPECT, TEST, AND SERVICE THE DISTRIBUTOR

All distributors—electronic as well as mechanical—should be inspected at each tune-up. In mechanical distributors, the contact breaker set, or points, should be replaced and adjusted. And when the points are replaced, replace the condenser. The condenser "fine tunes" the ignition spark so it jumps precisely at the correct instant and in the correct direction.

For all distributors equipped with vacuum advance, check the diaphragm for leaks and the linkage for binding and roughness, as described below. If the diaphragm leaks, you'll have to replace the vacuum chamber. The linkage can usually be fixed with a good cleaning and lubrication. Use a small file to remove burrs from the linkage, and lubricate it lightly with a silicon-base distributor cam grease. Don't use grease with a low melting point; engine heat will loosen it up, and it will be thrown all around and could get on the points. And don't use brake grease, because it can wear out the point cam.

GM-type distributor caps are held in place with spring-loaded L-hooks. Just press down on each hook, and turn it 90 degrees counter-clockwise. Another common way of holding the cap on is with two spring clips. Some imports use screws to attach the cap.

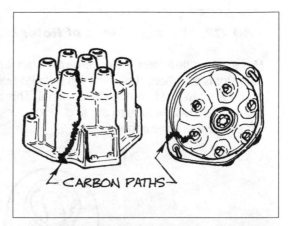

Inspect the distributor cap for damage and carbon tracking. *Cracks will allow moisture to get into the distributor, and can create erratic sparking. Carbon tracking is the result of high resistance. Replace the cap if either condition is present.*

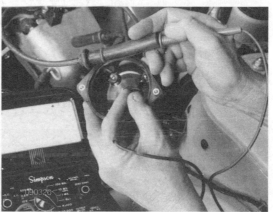

Measure the resistance of the cap contact with the wires installed. *Touch one probe to the contact in the spark plug boot and the other probe to the corresponding metal contact inside the cap. The cap is okay if resistance for all of the terminals is within a 10 percent range. If even one contact is very high, replace the cap.*

The metal tip of the distributor rotor should be bright and smooth. *A few strokes of a file will usually clean it up. However, if it's still rough, replace it. Check the mechanical advance mechanism by turning the rotor and releasing it. It should spring back. If it binds, a little WD-40 or a similar cleaner-lubricant should free it.*

PRO TIP: The Importance of Rotor Length

Make sure a new rotor is the correct length for the distributor cap. If the rotor is too short, the spark will have to bridge a large gap inside the cap just to reach the terminal. This produces a weak spark which results in hard starting, poor performance, and excessive fuel consumption.

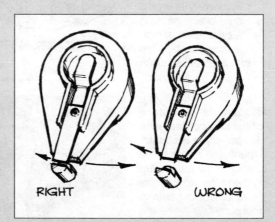

Too-short rotor creates another gap for the spark to jump.

RIGHT   WRONG

Check the vacuum-advance diaphragm. Disconnect the hose, move the breaker plate to full advance, cover the fitting, and release the plate. It should barely move. Then, uncover the fitting and the plate should snap back. If the diaphragm doesn't work, replace it. Take the old one to the parts store so you can match it with a new one.

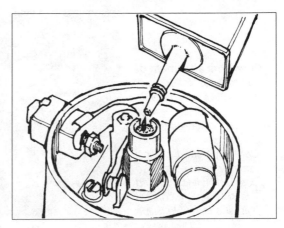

Oil the wick for the centrifugal advance mechanism. On many distributors, lubrication for the advance mechanism is provided by an oil wick inside the distributor shaft. Add a few drops of oil to ensure the advance mechanism will operate freely.

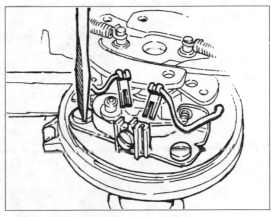

Remove the old points. Note the color of the wires and where they connect. On some GM distributors, the wires are held in place with spring tension. To remove the wires, carefully pry the spring open with a screwdriver.

Clean and grease the distributor cam. If the cam is worn it will affect timing. For many distributors, it's possible to replace just the cam. For others, the entire distributor must be replaced. If your distributor has a wick that lubes the cam, give it a couple of drops of engine oil—no more.

Check the alignment of the points. *Not only will correctly aligned points work their best, they will also last longer than if they are misaligned. Carefully bend the fixed point with needle-nose pliers until it lines up and is in complete contact with the movable point.*

Install new points and condenser. *Compare the new points to the old to make sure they are the same type. If there is a ground wire in the distributor, be sure to put it under one of the screw heads and not between the points and the breaker plate.*

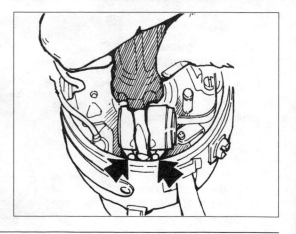

Make certain the condenser is correctly mounted and connected. *Make sure any tangs on the condenser bracket are correctly located in the distributor so the condenser won't interfere with the points.*

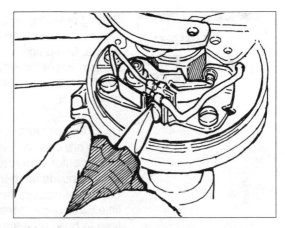

Most distributors use a screw to connect the primary coil wire to the spring. *For those GM distributors that don't have a screw, the wire terminal is held in place by spring pressure.*

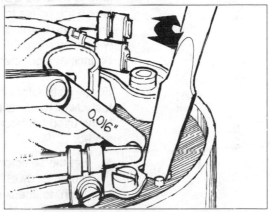

With the rubbing block of the new points on the peak of one of the cam lobes, set the initial gap. *Adjust the gap so there is a slight drag on the specified-size feeler gauge when it is drawn through the points. Tighten the holddown screws. The gap should be set more precisely with a dwell meter, as shown on the next pages.*

For GM V8 engines with single-point distributors, adjust the initial point gap by turning the Allen screw. *Turn the screw clockwise to decrease the gap, counterclockwise to increase it. The gap should be set more precisely with a dwell meter, as shown on the next pages.*

USING A TACH/DWELL METER

Setting point gap with a dwell meter is a more precise method than just using a flat feeler gauge. Manufacturers usually provide a gap measurement for initial point setting, and a dwell-angle specification for precise final adjustment.

Dwell angle refers to the amount of time the points are closed. It is expressed in degrees of distributor cam rotation. During this time, voltage builds up in the coil. The longer the points are closed, the greater the spark. Too little dwell angle doesn't give the coil enough time to build up a strong spark, plus it will cause the points to open slowly, resulting in arcing and burning. Too much dwell angle will cause rough idle, hard starting, and point bounce at high speed.

For all distributors the hookup of the tach/dwell meter is the same, whether it's being used to check dwell angle or engine speed:

■ Set the selector switch on the tach/dwell meter at "dwell" to check dwell angle or "tach" to check engine speed.

■ Connect the positive lead from the meter—usually red—to the negative terminal of the coil.

■ Connect the negative lead from the meter—usually black—to a good engine ground.

Crank the engine with a remote starter switch, and watch the dwell meter. The dwell angle should be the same as shown on your car's emission information sticker or in your shop manual. If it's not, loosen the point plate screw just enough so you can move the plate to correct the dwell angle. For *less* dwell angle, *increase* the gap. For *more* dwell angle, *decrease* the gap.

When checking and setting dwell angle, don't crank the engine for more than 10 seconds at a time. Otherwise, the starter may overheat and could be damaged.

Once the dwell angle is correct, tighten the screws in the point plate and recheck the dwell angle to make sure it didn't change.

Typical dwell meter hookup. The negative hookup goes to battery ground and the positive hookup goes to the negative terminal on the coil. Dwell angle on most distributors (all except some GM V8 engines) is adjusted by turning over the engine with the distributor cap off. Be sure to ground the coil high-tension wire. If you don't have an assistant, connect a remote starter switch (page 34).

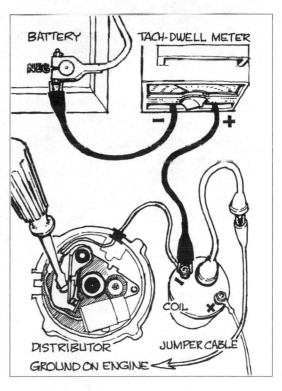

Dwell angle on GM V8's with distributor "window" may be adjusted with the engine running. To increase dwell angle, turn the Allen screw clockwise. To decrease dwell angle, turn the Allen screw counterclockwise.

Install the distributor cap and connect the spark plug wires. Double check the wires against the firing order to make sure they're connected in correct order so there's no chance of misfiring.

PRO TIP: Make Sure Ignition Polarity is Correct

If you replace a bad coil in an electronic ignition, leave it in place until you have connected the new coil, one lead at a time. This ensures that the polarity is correct.

If your engine is hard to start, misses at high speed, or quickly erodes the side electrodes on the spark plugs, your ignition polarity may be wrong. Check the wiring against a diagram for your engine, or reverse the coil leads and test drive the car. If it now starts easily and no longer misses at high speed, you have just corrected a problem that has been known to baffle some pros.

Breaker-point ignition: Checking for correct ignition polarity in a contact breaker ignition is easy: Just make sure the primary wire to the distributor connects to the negative pole on the coil.

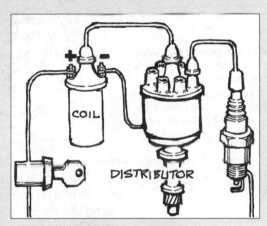

Electronic ignition: For an electronic ignition where the primary wire from the distributor first passes through an ICM (ignition control module), it isn't always easy to trace the wires to determine which is negative and which is positive.

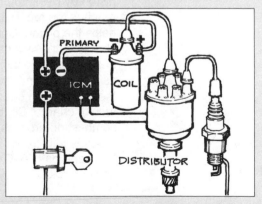

HOW TO CHECK AND ADJUST IGNITION TIMING

Ignition timing refers to the point at which the spark plug fires in relation to the position of the piston. Timing is expressed in degrees of crankshaft rotation relative to the piston at top-dead-center—TDC. For example, the timing specification for a 1990 Nissan Maxima is 15° before top-dead-center, or 15° BTDC.

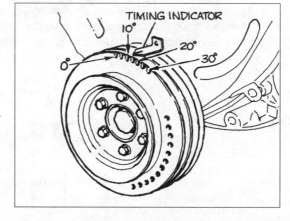

On this timing indicator the marks represent 5°.
Thus, when the mark on the pulley is lined up with the third mark before the "0," the timing is 15° BTDC.

What this means is that the spark plug fires 15 degrees *before* the piston reaches the top of its stroke on compression. This might sound like the spark is working against the piston by trying to drive it back down before it reaches the top, but the early spark actually helps the piston. Combustion of the fuel/air charge in the cylinder doesn't happen all at once. The explosion begins at the spark plug as a "flame front" that travels outward through the combustion chamber igniting all of the fuel/air charge. So, by starting the combustion process just a little early, it reaches full strength by the time the piston has gone past TDC and started down on the power stroke.

If ignition occurs too early, it will work against the piston. This occurrence is what is known as pre-ignition and is commonly called "knock," or "ping." If ignition occurs too late, combustion is slow and incomplete. This results in poor performance and is usually felt as sluggish acceleration and general lack of power.

The shapes of the combustion chamber and the top of the piston affect the speed of the flame front. And because automotive engines use many different designs, some require more or less ignition advance than others. This is why it's important that you adjust the ignition timing as specified on the underhood emissions label.

PRO TIP: Why Factory Timing is Best

There's a common myth that if you increase ignition advance over what the factory recommends, you will also increase power. Not true.

Here are the facts. From 6°-8° BTDC, performance increases just slightly more than 2%. Beyond 8° BTDC, performance begins to fall off, and fuel consumption increases. But more important, spark plug temperature and engine temperature climb rapidly to the point that serious damage can result.

PLUG TEMPERATURE
POWER OUTPUT

% INCREASE

2° 4° 6° 8° 10° 12°
TIMING OVER-ADVANCE (BTDC)

At each tune-up, you should check ignition timing—and adjust it if necessary. You're not likely to find large timing errors—just an occasional small one caused by normal wear. This important tune-up task takes just a few minutes. You will need a timing light, of course, and a wrench to loosen the distributor hold-down bolt. (A few high-tech engines do not have timing that is adjustable by turning the distributor. These engines use a very accurate computer to control timing under a wide range of engine speed and load.)

Connect the timing light.
With the engine shut off, connect the red wire from the timing light to the POS battery terminal. Connect the black wire to a good ground. And connect the induction pickup to the No. 1 spark plug wire. Make sure the timing light wires are clear of the cooling fan, drive belts and pulleys, and any other rotating parts.

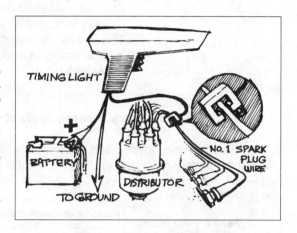

Determine the correct timing and idle speed.
You'll find this information on the emissions sticker under the hood or in your shop manual. Also note whether the distributor vacuum advance must be connected or disconnected when checking the timing.

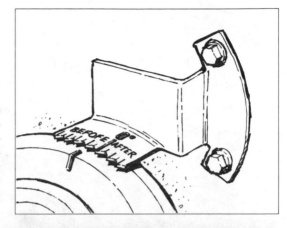

Locate the timing marks.
With few exceptions, they're located on the crankshaft damper on the front of the engine. Wipe grease and dirt off of the marks. Sometimes filling the marks with chalk or a light-colored crayon makes them easier to see.

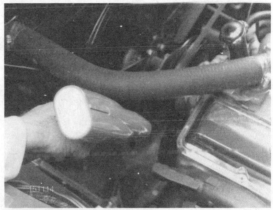

Check the timing. If necessary for your engine, disconnect the distributor vacuum hose from the carburetor and plug the port. Run the engine at idle. Point the light at the marks and press the trigger. The pulley mark should line up with the appropriate mark on the pointer when the light flashes.

Adjust the ignition timing. Loosen the distributor bolt located at the base of the distributor so you can turn the distributor. Then, slowly turn the distributor until the timing marks line up. Tighten the distributor bolt and recheck the timing. Then, shut off the engine, connect the vacuum hose, and disconnect the timing light.

Section 7:
Carburetor/ Fuel Injection

Back in the muscle-car days of the '60's, every proper tune-up included the black magic of numerous carburetor adjustments (and carburetor jetting for us go-fast guys). But for almost two decades the mixture screw has been sealed at the factory, and the only adjustment you can make to either a carburetor or fuel injection system is idle speed. (Frankly, that's all that is needed.)

The do-it-yourselfer still has much valuable (and money-saving) work he or she can do on modern engines. Today, the theme is to clean and inspect the system, and replace the air filter and fuel filter religiously.

HOW TO CLEAN THE CARBURETOR

If your engine has a carburetor, clean it regularly as shown below to avoid sticking linkage and sluggish performance. (You may also choose to use a can of gasoline additive if you suspect a problem.)

WARNING: Before using carburetor cleaner, read and understand the manufacturer's directions and warnings. Carburetor cleaner is potentially harmful if not used correctly.

Clean the outside of the carburetor. Remove the air cleaner case and note the location of any hoses you have to disconnect (see facing page). Spray carburetor cleaner liberally on the linkage to remove gummy deposits that can prevent the choke and throttle linkage from working properly.

Clean the carburetor choke and throttle plates and the air intake. Liberally spray carburetor cleaner into the air intake. Then start the engine, and let it idle as you spray more cleaner into the intake. When the engine hesitates, stop spraying until it smooths out, then continue to clean.

PRO TIP: Keeping Track of Vacuum Hoses

Many emission control systems have a number of vacuum and breather hoses connected to the air cleaner case. Each one has a specific purpose, and together they help your engine to run smoothly, efficiently, and pollution-free. Hook them up wrong and you're likely to experience rough idle, stalling, stumbling during acceleration, and terrible fuel economy. Sometimes, the engine won't even start.

To make sure this doesn't happen when you remove the air cleaner case from the engine, first make a simple numbered diagram of all the connection points. Then, as you disconnect each hose, mark it with a piece of tape on which you've written the connection point number from the diagram. (Or you can actually put a tape number right on the connection point.) When you're ready to install the case, all you have to do is match up the numbers.

This is a good time to replace vacuum hoses that are cracked or show other signs of deterioration. Use the old hose for a pattern and cut the new one to the same length.

Use tape with numbers to keep track of vacuum hoses. The number on the hose corresponds to the tape number near the connection point.

HOW TO CLEAN AND INSPECT THE FUEL INJECTION SYSTEM

One of the most important "cleaning" items for fuel injection systems is to use gasoline with specific cleaning additives for fuel injectors. According to *Consumer Reports* magazine, most *major* brands have these necessary additives. If you're not sure about the brand you buy, ask if it passes the "BMW test for fuel injectors."

If you suspect that an injector is not working properly, you might try a can of fuel injector cleaner in the fuel tank. (There's no guarantee that this will work, but it's inexpensive to try.)

Modern electronic fuel injection systems are extremely reliable. Since they are an integral part of the emissions control system for an engine, they must be covered by the manufacturer's 50,000-mile warranty. Some older (late 70's) European systems had problems with water corroding electrical connectors, which played havoc with the system. But you'll find that the modern ones from America, Japan, and Europe are all very well designed.

Perhaps the most important part of "inspecting" a fuel injection system is done *behind the wheel* rather than under the hood. Is your fuel-injected car or truck driving well? Does it start easily, warm-up properly, and run at highway speeds without surging? Have you noticed any drop off in power or driveability? If you have no problems, you can be 99.9% sure that the system is operating fine. Still, a peek under the hood can sometimes reveal a problem that's just getting underway.

Inspect the injectors closely for signs of fuel leakage. *Each cylinder has one injector. Fuel injection systems operate under a lot of internal pressure, and leaks can cause a real problem. Look for dark, hard-to-remove stains.*

Inspect the electrical connectors of the whole fuel injection system. *Make sure they are tightly fastened. If one has come loose, check it for any signs of corrosion. These wires send signals to the computer and control the injectors, so they are critically important.*

Inspect vacuum hoses for damage. *The system receives much of its operating information through these "data paths." If a vacuum hose leaks or is disconnected, the system may not be receiving a valuable piece of information, or a vital control valve may not operate as it should. Replace a bad hose as soon as you spot it.*

Clean the throttle linkage and the outside of the fuel injection system. *Use carburetor cleaner. Again, look closely for any sign of gasoline leakage. (If it's necessary to remove the air cleaner, keep track of the hoses and wires, as shown on page 69.)*

If you find any signs of fuel leakage or loose connectors, have the system checked out by a qualified technician specializing in fuel injection systems. Fuel leaks in a pressurized fuel-injection system pose a serious fire hazard. Unless you are an expert with special training, test equipment, and factory manuals, repairs can really get botched. (The authors have written several official factory training programs for dealership technicians on diagnosis and repair of electronic fuel injection systems. Trust us on this advice!)

The final—and critical—part of fuel injection system maintenance is replacing the fuel filter, as explained on the next page. You may have gotten by with ignoring this bit of maintenance on your carbureted engines, but failing to replace the fuel filter on a fuel-injected engine will result in a very expensive repair. Count on it.

HOW TO REPLACE THE FUEL FILTER(S)

Regular replacement of the fuel filter(s) is critical to proper engine operation and long life. Failing to replace a filter can allow it to get clogged with sediment, and shut off the fuel flow to your engine.

Carbureted engines usually have one fuel filter under the hood. Trace the fuel line back from the carburetor to locate it.

Fuel-injected engines also usually have one fuel filter under the hood, located in the line to the fuel distribution manifold. But check the maintenance schedule in your Owner's Manual (or ask a dealership service writer) if you have more than one fuel filter. Sometimes, there is a second filter near the gas tank.

Fuel-injection systems are under pressure. That pressure must be relieved before replacing the fuel filter(s). See the *Pro Tip* on page 75 for the most common procedure. If in doubt, check with a qualified technician or model-specific shop manual.

In-line fuel filter replacement tips: Install with new soft connector hoses of the correct diameter. Make sure the flow arrow is pointed in the direction of fuel flow—toward the carburetor or fuel-injection manifold.

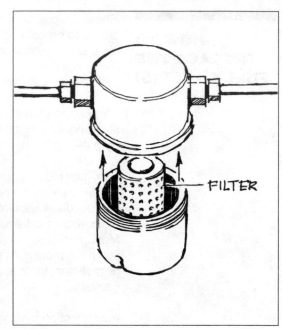

FILTER

Canister filter replacement tips: These are usually mounted with hard metal lines. Unscrew the canister, remove the old filter element, clean inside the canister, and install a new filter. If the canister gasket is hard or cracked, replace it.

PRO TIP: Special Handling for Fuel Injection Filters

WARNING: Fuel injection systems operate under pressure, some of which will remain even when the engine is shut off. Before you can safely remove the old fuel filter, you must first relieve that pressure. Otherwise, gasoline will spray out of the fuel lines and create a dangerous fire hazard. Here's how to relieve the pressure:

1. With the engine idling, remove the fuel pump fuse. This will stop the fuel pump and kill the engine. Most important: this will relieve the pressure in the fuel system.

3. Disconnect the hoses from the fuel filter. Keep flame and sparks away. Gasoline is highly flammable.

4. Replace the hoses if they are cracked, swollen, or damaged.

5. Connect the fuel lines to the new fuel filter. (Don't reuse the old clamps.) Tighten the new clamps firmly.

6. To prevent engine from starting, unplug coil wire from distributor cap (or primary plug to control box on electronic ignition).

7. Install the fuel pump fuse.

8. Turn the engine over for several seconds, and check for leaks.

9. Reconnect the coil wire or primary plug. You're done!

With the engine idling, removing the fuel pump fuse will deactivate the pump and relieve fuel pressure. Remember to put the fuse back after the new filter has been installed.

HOW TO INSPECT AND TEST THE PCV SYSTEM

The PCV (positive crankcase ventilation) valve is your engine's most basic emission control device. It allows combustion gases and oil fumes in the crankcase to be drawn into the cylinders and burned.

The PCV valve eventually becomes clogged with carbon and oil, causing rough running. Therefore, you should test it every time you do a tune-up, and replace it when it's clogged.

The PCV valve is usually located on the valve cover and is connected to the base of the carburetor or intake manifold with a rubber hose. Some valves screw into the cover and others are simply held in place with a rubber grommet.

Test the PCV valve for suction. Run the engine at idle. Disconnect the valve from the engine, and cover the end of the valve. If there is strong vacuum, the valve is good. If vacuum is weak or there isn't any, the valve may be blocked. However, before replacing the valve, make sure the hose isn't blocked.

HOW TO REPLACE THE AIR FILTER

This is one of the most important jobs that the do-it-yourselfer can do. Regular air filter replacement prolongs the life of your engine and gives you better performance and gas mileage. Air filters are inexpensive and very easy to replace. We do *not* recommend that you clean an air filter. This was a common practice in the distant past, but today air filters are quite inexpensive, and they are designed to filter finer particles. If you're going to invest your time, put a few bucks into a new filter, and do the job right! Shown below are a few typical air filter installations.

The most common type: a round filter on top of a carburetor. This type of cover is usually held in place with a wingnut in the center. There may also be spring clips to undo at several points around the edge of the cover.

Clean the filter case thoroughly after removing the old filter. This ensures that dirt dislodged from the old filter won't find its way into the engine.

If your filter case has a PCV filter like this one, replace it when you replace the air filter. The PCV filter removes oil vapor from the air that's drawn through the crankcase ventilation system and into the carburetor.

Many fuel-injected engines have "remote" air filters. The filter case (arrow) is connected to the fuel-injection system with a length of stiff plastic hose.

To replace this type of filter, unhook the snaps that secure the cover, and pull out the old filter element. Clean the inside of the case before installing the new filter. Also, look for arrows or the word "UP" that shows you how to correctly install the new element.

HOW TO ADJUST IDLE SPEED

You will find the recommended idle speed on the emission sticker in the engine compartment. Read the sticker carefully. If you have an automatic transmission, note whether it should be in Drive or Park. If you have power steering, the pump can load the engine unless you point the front wheels straight ahead.

Idle speed that is too fast can cause excessive brake wear and automatic transmission overheating. Idle speed that is too slow can cause the engine to die when you come to a stop in traffic. Altitude and temperature affect idle speed more on carbureted engines than on fuel-injected engines, which often have automatic compensation for these factors.

In adjusting idle speed, you are actually adjusting the throttle opening. You adjust the amount of air, and the carburetor or fuel-injection system adjusts the amount of fuel. Obviously, this adjustment should be done *after* you have replaced the air cleaner and have the case reassembled.

Warm up the engine to normal operating temperature. This is critically important since all engines idle faster when cold. Drive the vehicle for several miles, until the temperature is normal.

Connect your tach/dwell meter as shown on page 59. Set the switch for tachometer operation. If your tach/dwell meter has a scale selector, switch to the expanded scale for accurate measurement at low rpm's. Most dash-board tachometers are not accurate enough for setting idle speed.

Carburetors: The idle speed adjustment screw is on the throttle linkage. Turn the screw slowly to get idle speed exactly right.

Fuel Injection: Idle speed adjustment screw is usually on the throttle body. Often, your Owner's Manual will show the location if you can't spot it immediately. If the throttle linkage on your fuel injection does not have an idle adjustment screw, don't worry; the idle is controlled electronically and is not designed to be adjusted.

OLDIES ONLY: FAST IDLE AND MIXTURE

If your car or truck was built in the 60's or before, there is a good chance you have two more adjustments on your carburetor: idle mixture and fast idle speed. The idle mixture screw regulates the amount of gas that flows through the carburetor idle circuit. The fast idle speed adjustment sets engine speed for warm-up right after a cold start. The correct order for these adjustments is (1) curb idle speed, (2) idle mixture, and (3) fast idle speed.

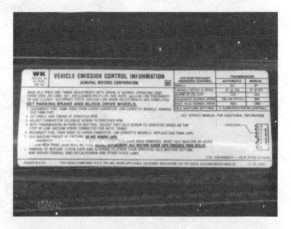

To know for sure whether you need to adjust fast idle speed or idle mixture, check your underhood emissions label. If either number is specified, chances are you need to make an adjustment as part of your tune up.

Hook up your tach/dwell meter as shown on page 59. If your tach/dwell meter has a scale selector, switch to the expanded scale for accurate measurement at low rpm's.

Adjust curb idle speed.
The screw is on the throttle linkage. Set it for the normal low speed specified on the emissions label.

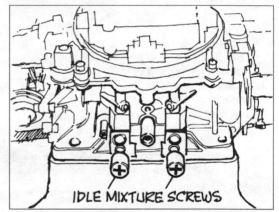

Adjust the idle mixture.
This screw is in the base of the carburetor. Turn the mixture screw slowly in until the engine speed begins to drop. Then back it out until the rpm is highest, and stop. If there are two idle mixture screws, do this for each one.

IDLE MIXTURE SCREWS

Adjust fast-idle speed.
First rotate the fast-idle cam so the fast-idle screw rests on the step specified on the emissions label. Then turn the fast-idle screw on the throttle linkage to set the correct speed. This is usually around 900-1100 rpm. Make sure you observe all conditions specified on the emissions label.

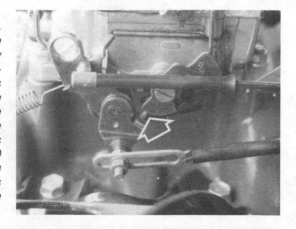

ROAD TEST—THE QUALITY CHECK

Here is where your hard work is rewarded. If you've done everything right, your car or truck will deliver all the performance and economy that were designed into it.

Begin by starting the engine and checking for smooth idle. If idle is rough, shut off the engine and check all spark plug connections. Double check to make sure you haven't mixed up any of the wires. Then try again. If rough idle persists, recheck ignition timing.

Once the engine idles smoothly, test drive the car. Listen and feel for unfamiliar sounds and sensations. Accelerate briskly. The engine should pull strong and smooth with no hesitation or dead spots.

If the engine knocks, or "pings," excessively during acceleration, you will probably have to retard the timing slightly. If pinging still persists, try changing gasoline brands. All refinery blends are not the same. An equivalent gasoline from a brand other than the one you are presently using may eliminate the pinging.

Check for smooth idle when you come to a stop. If the car has an automatic transmission, it should idle smoothly in gear and then accelerate without hesitation.

Back home, shut off the engine, wait a few seconds, and restart it. It should start immediately and idle smoothly.

Part B:
Electrical Service

MORE GOLDEN RULES OF CAR AND TRUCK MAINTENANCE

- Learn and understand. Let each job that you master build a foundation for your next.

- Be kind to Planet Earth. Recycle used batteries and drained oil. Check with local auto parts stores and service stations. Don't poison your children and grandchildren.

- Take care of your tools and manuals. Store them so they are ready to go the next time.

- Enjoy. Most of us perform do-it-yourself work to save money. But as your skills grow, you will often do the job faster, better, and more conveniently than if you used a professional mechanic.

Section 8:
Electrical Parts, Supplies, and Tools

The parts, supplies, and tools shown here are needed for the electrical service and troubleshooting jobs described in this book. These jobs apply to old cars and trucks as well as new.

Check the specific job you want to do to see what's needed. Buy only what you need, and let your collection grow as you save money over a period of time.

We recommend that you invest in good quality tools. They make your work more enjoyable and often are cheaper in the long run because they last longer.

Electrical Service

Volt/ohmmeter—Also called a multimeter or a VOM. This tool is essential for most electrical troubleshooting. You will use it for measuring ignition wire resistance, battery and lighting circuit voltage, and continuity. A very inexpensive VOM is adequate for DIY automotive work.

Hydrometer—This will tell you the relative condition of the cells in a battery with removable caps—or the overall condition of a sealed battery with a test port.

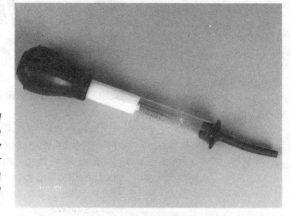

Battery post cleaning tool—This removes corrosion from top-mounted battery posts and terminals to ensure good connections.

Baking soda—*Acid deposits that build up on the battery and its terminals are quickly neutralized with baking soda.*

Distilled water—*This is essential for replenishing the electrolyte in serviceable batteries. While tap water can be used in a pinch, the impurities it contains can shorten battery life.*

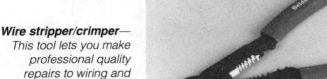

Wire stripper/crimper—*This tool lets you make professional quality repairs to wiring and connectors. Cheapo models work okay, but we like the better quality units that are actually easier to use.*

Assortment of connectors and terminals—*These are used for wiring repairs as well as for accessory installation.*

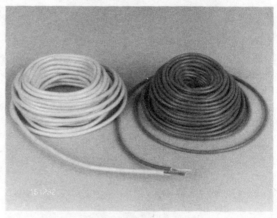

Electrical wire—14 and 18 gauge—*These two wire sizes will cover most electrical repair situations and accessory installations in cars and trucks.*

Electrical tape—*You'll need this to protect repairs and connectors from shorting or grounding, plus it keeps your work tidy.*

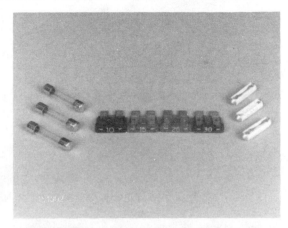

Assorted fuses—*Keep a couple each of 10-amp, 15-amp, 20-amp, and 30-amp fuses in the glove compartment. When you need them you really need them. Make sure you buy the correct type for each vehicle in the family.*

Lamp bulbs—*A good selection to carry in your vehicle would include tail/stop lamp bulbs, directional lamp bulbs, and headlamp bulb. Your Owner's Manual should list bulb specifications.*

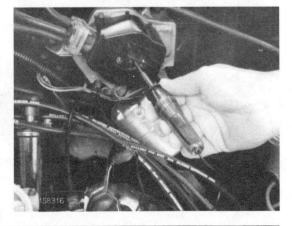

Test lamp—*This handy tool relies on current in the system to light it. If current is present, the lamp lights. No current, no light. It couldn't be simpler. The pointed probe can pierce insulation to make contact with a wire or reach down into connectors to make contact with the pins.*

Section 9:

Battery

The battery in your car or truck may look like a pretty simple device—just a big plastic box where you store electricity. But don't be fooled; the battery is a virtual electro-chemical factory that is at work around the clock, even when your vehicle is parked.

A battery doesn't need a lot of maintenance, but what it *does* need is important. Since a "dead battery" can leave you stranded, the advice given in this section is especially important. That is, unless you enjoy exploring strange places and meeting new people in the middle of the night!

Read on. Knowing what goes on inside your battery will help you better understand the care it needs.

WHAT A BATTERY IS MADE OF

Inside that plastic box are several dozen vertical plates suspended in a solution of water and sulfuric acid. This solution is called *electrolyte*.

There are two types of plates—negative plates that contain pure sponge lead, and positive plates that contain lead dioxide. The plates are grouped into sets called *cells,* which are alternated negative, positive, negative, positive, and so on.

Each cell is an individual battery that produces 2 volts, and six of these, in series, produce 12 volts.

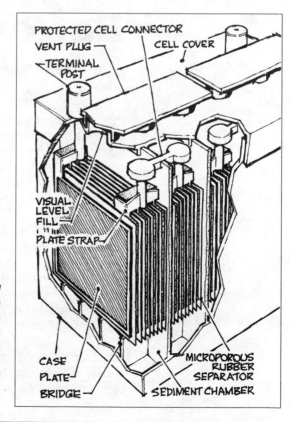

This is typical construction for an automotive battery. *The sediment chamber in the bottom of the case allows the buildup of deposits that slough off of the plates normally throughout the battery's life.*

PROTECTED CELL CONNECTOR
VENT PLUG
CELL COVER
TERMINAL POST
VISUAL LEVEL FILL
PLATE STRAP
CASE
PLATE BRIDGE
MICROPOROUS RUBBER SEPARATOR
SEDIMENT CHAMBER

HOW A BATTERY WORKS

The lead compounds on the plates react with the acid solution, resulting in electron flow from one type of plate to the other.

For example, when you complete the circuit to the starter, electrons flow from the negative plates to the positive plates, creating a current that drives the starter motor. This process—discharging—also changes the lead compounds and uses up the electrical energy.

To restore the electrical energy, the electron flow must be reversed. This process—charging—is what happens when the alternator supplies current to the battery.

WHAT CAN GO WRONG WITH A BATTERY

Other than being dropped or hit hard, the worst thing that can happen to a battery is to allow it to discharge completely. Repeated deep discharging will cause a battery to fail prematurely. Deep discharging causes the crystalline lead structure of the plates to break down, and it can cause internal contact paths (short circuits) to develop between positive and negative plates. Such damage

To test the battery for internal shorting with a voltmeter, touch the positive meter lead to the positive battery terminal and the negative meter lead to the negative battery terminal. A good battery will indicate at least 12 volts. If the reading is substantially less, even after a recent charge, replace it.

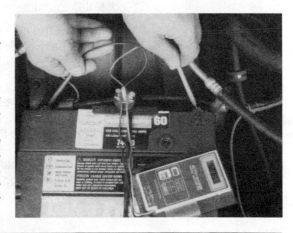

disables one or more cells and ruins the battery. Rarely does this happen to all cells at the same time. Usually, a weak battery has just one or two bad cells.

To check a battery for dead cells, begin by fully charging it. Next, apply a brief load, such as turning on the headlamps for a few seconds. Then measure the voltage across the terminals as shown on the preceding page. If the voltmeter shows 12 or more volts, the battery is okay. However, if it shows 10 volts or less, it's a safe bet that the battery has internal shorting.

Despite what you may have heard, you can't recondition a shorted battery by turning it upside down and thumping it on the ground. The battery must be replaced.

HOW TO MAKE A BATTERY LAST

During the normal process of charging and discharging, small amounts of electrolyte are consumed and the crystalline structure of the lead plates in the battery slowly break down. This is what eventually causes the battery to "wear out." To make a battery last as long as possible, you must:

1. **Maintain the correct electrolyte level** by occasionally adding pure or distilled water. Avoid using water with high mineral content.

2. **Never allow the battery to discharge fully.** Simply driving your car once a week or more will keep the battery charged.

If you must store your car, connect a battery charger to it every couple of weeks and charge it at a low amperage rate overnight.

HOW TO SERVICE THE BATTERY

Many modern batteries are referred to as "maintenance free." Generally, this type is sealed and doesn't require the addition of water. Some, however, are "maintenance accessible," and will allow for the addition of water (see manufacturer's instructions). The more conventional refillable type is still prevalent—and is preferred by many experts. But whether "maintenance-free" or not, *all batteries require some service.*

A critical part of regular battery service is disconnecting the cables and cleaning the cable ends and battery terminals. When the cables are disconnected, electrical power is cut off to *all* electrical systems in the vehicle. If you have an electronic radio with preset stations, the memory may be erased when the battery is disconnected. Thus, it's a good idea to write down your radio station numbers before you disconnect the battery, so you can easily reprogram your radio after the battery is reconnected. And, if you have an owner-programmable alarm, remember to reprogram it as well, or your vehicle will be without theft protection.

This maintenance-free battery is sealed. Water can't be added to it. The "eye" on the top indicates charge level—green means full charge, no color means discharge.

Electrical Service

This battery has removable caps. Water can be added when the electrolyte level is low. Also, each of this battery's six cells can be individually checked to troubleshoot suspected battery problems.

WARNING: A battery emits highly explosive hydrogen gas during charging. The precautions below must be followed to ensure your safety. If you fail to follow these warnings, the battery could explode and cause serious injury.

- Do not smoke or have an open flame while working near the battery.

- Do not lay a tool across the top of the battery. It could bridge the terminals and cause a spark.

- Take care when lifting the battery—it's heavy.

- Wear safety goggles while working with the battery. Battery acid can injure your eyes.

- If you spill battery acid on yourself, your clothing, or the vehicle, rinse it off immediately with large amounts of water. Battery acid is corrosive.

Neglected batteries have ways of showing their displeasure. High-resistance acid deposits build up on the terminals, and will eventually result in poor starting or in no starting at all. Low water level results in complete failure of the battery.

Simple, periodic battery maintenance can head off this sort of trouble before it occurs. Regular maintenance will allow your battery to live a dependable life and reach a ripe old age!

Here's what you will need to service your battery—a 10-mm or 1/2-inch combination wrench, a battery post-and cable cleaning tool, baking soda and water, a toothbrush, and petroleum jelly.

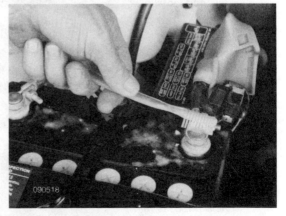

Clean the top of the battery. Neutralize gray acid deposits with a mixture of baking soda and water. Then, rinse off the battery and the area around it and under it with a gentle stream of clean water. Don't splash the solution onto the paint. If you should, rinse it off immediately.

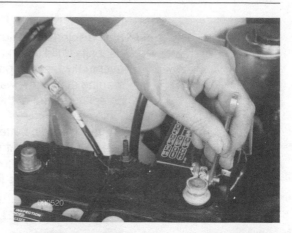

Disconnect the battery cables. *Disconnect the negative cable first, then the positive cable. Doing it in this order reduces the possibility of creating sparks.*

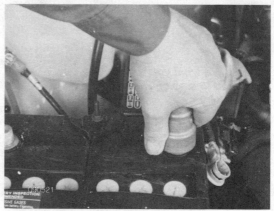

Clean the battery posts. *If you are using a terminal cleaning tool, twist it several times until the posts are shiny—they don't have to be smooth. A pen knife or medium-grit sandpaper can also be used to clean the posts and terminals.*

Side-terminal batteries need cleaning too. *Clean the terminals and the cable connectors with a wire brush, and neutralize acid deposits with baking soda.*

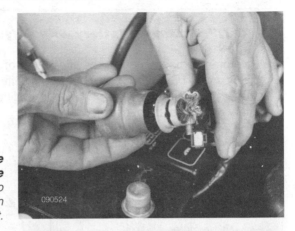

Clean inside the cable ends until they are shiny. *They don't have to be smooth—just clean and bright.*

Check the electrolyte level. *The level for all cells should be between the level lines on a translucent case (or above the plates in a black-case battery). If the level is low, fill the cells with pure or distilled water up to the upper level line on a translucent case (or to the bottom of each cell opening on a black case).*

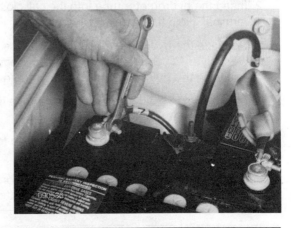

Connect the cables and protect the terminals. *Connect the positive cable first, then the negative. Tighten the bolts securely. Coat the terminals with petroleum jelly to retard corrosion. Then, reset the radio, alarm, and clock, as necessary.*

Electrical Service

A hydrometer measures the specific gravity of the electrolyte solution in the battery's cells. A specific gravity reading of 1.300 indicates a fully charged battery. Lower readings indicate a weak battery or a low state of charge.

To see what condition your battery is in, check each cell with a hydrometer, and compare the results to the Quick-Check Table on the facing page. Before you begin, make a sketch of the top of the battery so you can record the hydrometer readings for each cell. Be sure to follow the safety precautions on page 98.

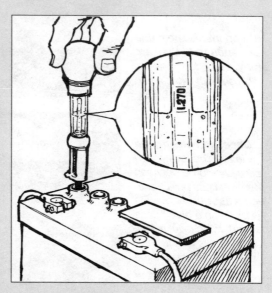

1. Remove the caps from the battery cells (or test port).

2. Insert the hydrometer tube into the cell closest to the positive terminal. Hold the hydrometer vertically.

3. Squeeze the hydrometer bulb, and release it slowly to draw in electrolyte. When the hydrometer float begins to rise, stop releasing the bulb. Keep the hydrometer in the cell.

4. Bend down to read the hydrometer at eye level. Write the number on your battery sketch.

5. Squeeze the bulb to return the electrolyte to the cell, and withdraw the hydrometer.

6. Check the other cells—in order—and record the readings. Then, use the facing table to determine your battery's condition.

Step 1: Hydrometer Corrections for Temperature

Use this table to correct your hydrometer readings for the temperature of the electrolyte. Write the corrected number for each cell on your sketch. (You will obtain greatest accuracy if the electrolyte is between 70 and 90°F.)

Temperature of electrolyte, °F	Add or subtract	Temperature of electrolyte, °F	Add or subtract
160	+.032	70	-.004
150	+.028	60	-.008
140	+.024	50	-.012
130	+.020	40	-.016
120	+.016	30	-.020
110	+.012	20	-.024
100	+.008	10	-.028
90	+.004	0	-.032
80	.000		

Step 2: Determine Battery Condition

Use the temperature-corrected specific gravity numbers you calculated above.

Difference between highest and lowest cells	Specific gravity of lowest cell @ 80°F as corrected	Battery condition
Less than 50 points	More than 1.230	Good, and satisfactorily charged.
Less than 50 points	Less than 1.230	Good, but needs charging.
More than 50 points	—	Defective. Should be replaced.

HOW TO REPLACE THE BATTERY

Most automotive batteries need to be replaced every two to five years. The telltale signs:

- Engine starter turns slower than usual.

- Headlights get dim when engine idles.

- Battery revives with charge, but doesn't hold for more than a day or two.

Before you replace your battery, check out the charging system (page 140) and check the battery (preceding two pages). But if you need a new one, here's how to replace it.

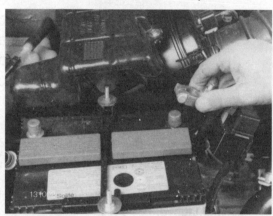

Disconnect both cables from the battery—first the negative and then the positive. Set them to the sides of the battery so they do not accidentally restore contact.

Remove the battery holddown clamp. Many clamps grip the battery near the base. For the type shown, with long J-bolts and a crossbar, loosen the nuts enough to let you disconnect the J-bolts from the battery tray. Make sure you have a firm hold on the battery before lifting it out of the case.

Clean the battery tray. *Scrub the tray with a baking soda solution. Flush the tray and surrounding areas with a gentle stream of clear water. If necessary, paint any exposed metal with rust-inhibiting paint.*

Install the new battery and the holddown clamp. *Tighten the bolt or nuts enough to prevent the battery from moving but not so tight that you crack the battery case.*

To finish the job, clean the battery cable terminals thoroughly before connecting them.

To minimize the danger of an accidental spark, connect the cable to the positive terminal first. Then connect the negative (ground) cable. Finally, coat the terminals with petroleum jelly to inhibit the buildup of acid deposits.

PRO TIP: How to Select a Replacement Battery

When buying a new battery, the first rule to follow is this: *make sure your new battery meets or exceeds the Cold Cranking Amperage (CCA) rating of the original battery.* (See the Pro Tip on page 112 for a full explanation.) The old rule of thumb was to select a battery with a CCA rating that equals or exceeds the engine's displacement in cubic inches. This worked pretty well with V-8s 20 years ago, but modern 4 and 6 cylinder electronic fuel injected engines need more battery power. Thus, the OEM battery capacity is a better guide.

In addition to CCA rating, make sure the replacement battery has the same terminal configuration (side post or top post) as the battery currently installed in the vehicle. If, for example, your car currently has a side-post battery, your battery cables won't fit a top-post battery unless you use special adapters — which we most definitely do *not* recommend. And while you're under the hood checking the type of terminals on your current battery, check out the size of the battery tray and the type of hold-down used to secure it in place. (Most cars and trucks leave the factory with a tray large enough to accomodate a larger, optional battery.) Your goal is simply to avoid installation "surprises" with your new replacement battery.

Happily, there is an easy way to select the correct battery. In the battery department you'll find a battery application and replacement book. If you don't see one in plain view, ask a salesperson for it. This book usually shows you several correct replacement choices for your vehicle's make, model and year. The batteries will vary in CCA power, "maintenance-free" or conventional design, price, and warranty. You may find that batteries of several different "Groups," or sizes, are offered; but any of the selections specified in the book should fit your battery tray, cables, and hold-down system. If you're planning on keeping your car or truck for more than a year or so, we think an upgraded battery is usually worth the extra dollars for the added life, capacity, and peace-of-mind that it offers.

Top terminals and side terminals require different cable connectors. All battery sizes and ratings are available with either type of terminals. Be sure your replacement battery matches your current type.

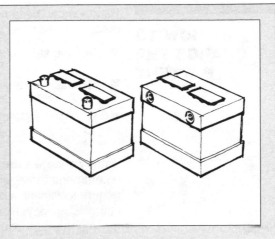

Your new battery should fit the vehicle's battery tray and hold-downs. If it's too large it won't fit in the tray, and if it's too small you may have trouble securing it. If your vehicle uses a side clamp to hold the battery in place, be certain the new battery is designed to be used with a side clamp.

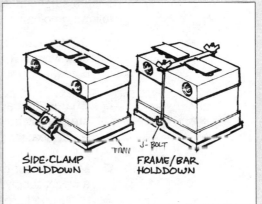

SIDE-CLAMP HOLDDOWN   FRAME/BAR HOLDDOWN   "J"-BOLT

HOW TO CHARGE THE BATTERY

Batteries can become discharged for a number of reasons:

- Vehicle stored for a long period of time.

- Excessive cranking trying to start engine.

- Charging system problems (see page 140).

Battery chargers are fairly inexpensive. We recommend those with an automatic charging feature to minimize overcharging. Battery charging is easy. However, you *must* follow the important precautions on page 98 to ensure safety. In addition, observe the following points:

- Do not hook up charger cables backwards. Reverse connection can damage the vehicle's alternator.

- Charge the battery in a well-ventilated area, away from open flames such as water heater pilot lights.

- Move the car to a well-drained area near a water supply. You'll be flushing the underhood area with water.

- Clean and service the battery as described on pages 97-103. It's essential that all the cells are full and the terminals are clean before charging.

- If you are using a 10-amp or smaller charger, leave the cell caps on the battery. If you are using a larger charger, follow the manufacturer's instructions regarding whether cell caps should be removed.

Connect the charger to the battery. *Make sure the battery charger is turned off and unplugged. First, connect the red cable clip from the charger to the POSITIVE battery post, then the black cable clip to the NEGATIVE post. Twist the clips on the posts to ensure good connections.*

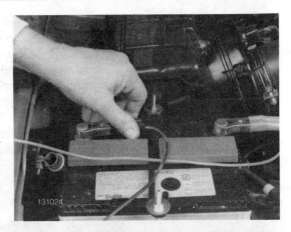

Plug in the charger and set the charge rate. *Follow the operating instructions for the battery charger to select the output and charging time. As a rule of thumb, a partially discharged battery should be charged about 4 hours. A fully discharged battery should be charged at least 8 hours.*

When charging is complete, unplug and disconnect the charger. *Unplug the power supply before you disconnect the cable clips—negative first, then positive.*

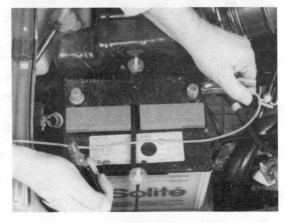

HOW TO REPLACE BATTERY CABLES

Normal corrosion will eventually erode away battery cables at the connections. This type of wear can become so great that the cable won't handle the load required by the starter. This condition is particularly common on the positive cable.

Check your cables for corrosion as well as damage to the insulation each time you service the battery. Replace cables before they erode all the way through and leave you stranded.

This cable is ready for retirement. Not only is it severely eroded, but the terminal has been beat on and tightened so much it's distorted and doesn't fit the post. And if that weren't enough, the insulation near the starter has been burned away by the exhaust pipe.

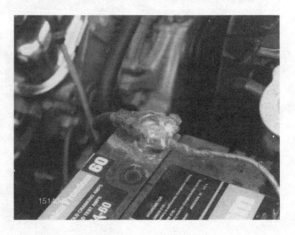

Cables are available in varying lengths at about 4-inch increments: 24, 28, 32 inches, etc. Also, if the old cables have "pigtails," so must the new ones. They are an essential part of your wiring. If necessary, make a sketch to take with you to the store to get the correct replacement. Here's how to measure the cables and install them.

Measure the old cable on the vehicle. Use a piece of string as a "pattern," then measure it to get the correct length for the new cable. Route the new cable alongside the old one to make sure it doesn't get in the way of suspension, exhaust pipes, etc. Then, remove the old cables.

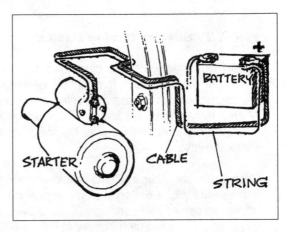

Connect the new cables in correct order. 1. Positive cable to starter solenoid. 2. Ground cable to engine. 3. Positive cable to POS battery post, and "pigtail" to terminal block. 4. Ground cable to NEG battery post, and "pigtail" to ground point. Protect the end of the new cables with petroleum jelly.

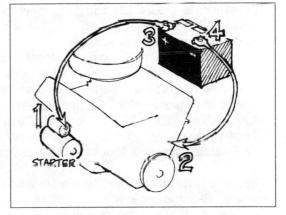

Electrical Service

PRO TIP: Battery Buying Basics

Battery manufacturers, like most folks in the automotive industry, have their own language to describe their products. Nevertheless, the characteristics these terms refer to are important considerations when purchasing a new battery. So, in the interest of making you a smart battery shopper, we offer the following quick course in how to speak battery.

Cold-Cranking Amps (CCA)—Cold-cranking amps is the measurement of a battery's ability to provide high current (amps) under extremely cold conditions. The CCA test measures the amperage delivered by a battery at 0°F (-18°C) for 30 seconds. A CCA rating of around 525-550 is sufficient for all but the coldest climates. A high CCA rating (625-630) is desirable for those locales where sub-freezing temperatures are common. But a battery with a higher CCA rating may also have thinner plates and a higher operating temperature, which will shorten its life. Here's a case where more isn't always better. In fact, some auto manufacturers are moving toward lower CCA ratings to improve battery life. In addition, you will find 32°F CCA ratings becoming more common. As compared to the 0°F CCA rating, the same CCA number for a 32°F rating represents about 15 - 20% less power in the battery.

Reserve Capacity (RC)—This term refers to a battery's "staying power." Reserve capacity is the maximum length of time, in minutes, that you can travel at night with minimum electrical load (25 amps) and no output from the alternator. Thus, a battery with a reserve capacity rating of 60 is good for 1 hour of night driving with the lights on—and with the heater blower motor or air-conditioning turned off. The higher the RC rating the better protection you have.

Deep Cycle—This term refers to a type of battery that can be repeatedly discharged and recharged and still perform like it's supposed to. Deep-cycle batteries are primarily for marine and recreational-vehicle use where recharging is done with a low-rate trickle charger. They are not good batteries for use in cars and trucks with high-rate charging systems.

Section 10:

Lamps and Wiring

It's not uncommon for bulbs to occasionally burn out. However, when the bulb in the same lamp has to be replaced frequently, look for a problem.

Wiring should last for the life of the car. However, problems can arise from chafed, cut, or burned insulation, or loose or corroded connectors. Or, you may simply wish to add an electrical accessory that requires splicing into your car's wiring.

This section shows you how to replace both sealed-beam and quartz-halogen headlamps and how to replace other bulbs. It shows you how to troubleshoot the most common problems. And it shows you how to repair wiring problems with professional results.

HOW TO REPLACE SEALED-BEAM HEADLAMP BULBS

There are two types of headlamp bulbs in use today. The most common is still the old sealed-beam type, in which the lens and filament are integrated into a single unit.

Sealed-beam lamp bulbs are usually removed from the front, after removing a trim bezel, then the bulb retainer ring, and unplugging the bulb from its socket.

The following photos show you how a typical replacement is done.

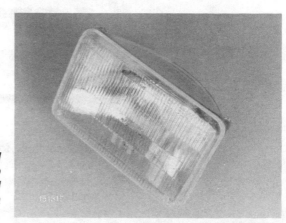

This is a typical sealed-beam headlamp bulb. The filament and reflector are sealed in a large one-piece unit.

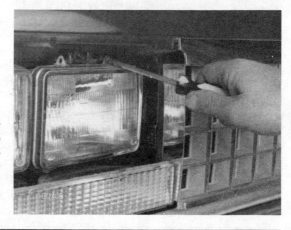

Sealed-beam headlamps are usually held in place with a retainer ring like this. In most cases, you must first remove a trim bezel. Don't disturb the adjustment screws.

To replace sealed-beam headlamps, first remove corrosion from the socket. Spray the socket with WD-40. Plug and unplug it from the old bulb several times to expose bright metal and ensure a good contact with the new bulb.

Make sure the new bulb is lined up with the headlamp "bucket." Knobs on the bulb fit into recesses in the bucket to ensure the beam is pointed in the right direction. Remember to connect the socket. Install the retainer and then the bezel.

WARNING: If your headlamps are the pop-up type, check your owner's manual for the correct and safe way to change the bulbs. It's possible for the lamps to suddenly retract without warning. If your hands are in the way you could be injured. If you cannot find instructions for your car, turn on the headlamps to raise them. Then, with the lamps up, disconnect the negative battery cable. In most cases this will ensure that the lamps won't retract.

HOW TO REPLACE QUARTZ-HALOGEN HEADLAMP BULBS

In recent years, the two-piece European-style quartz-halogen headlamp has come into common use in new domestic cars as well as imports from Asia and Europe. These bulbs are much easier to replace than sealed-beam bulbs because they simply plug into the back of the lamp reflector. They are usually held in place with a twist lock.

Typical two-piece quartz-halogen lamp assembly. *The bulb and reflector are separate components.*

Most two-piece quartz-halogen lamp bulbs are removed from the rear of the reflector. *Unplug the wires and free the bulb by turning it or a lock-ring counter-clockwise. Then pull the bulb out of the reflector. Just reverse these steps to install the new bulb.*

Do not touch the glass of a new quartz-halogen bulb with your bare hands. Use a clean rag or paper towel to hold the new bulb. Even a slight film of natural body oil will contaminate the bulb and cause it to burn out prematurely. If you do touch the glass, clean it with denatured alcohol or lacquer thinner to remove any oil.

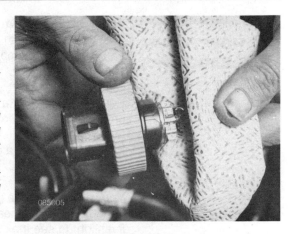

PRO TIP: How to Upgrade Conventional Tungsten Headlamps to Quartz-Halogen Bulbs

Sealed one-piece quartz-halogen replacement bulbs are available for virtually all cars and trucks that use conventional tungsten sealed-beam lamps. Quartz-halogen bulbs are more expensive than conventional sealed-beam bulbs, but they are much brighter. They connect and fit just like conventional sealed-beam bulbs.

In four-lamp installations, make sure you select the correct replacements and don't wind up with four high-beam-only lamps.

Quartz-halogen replacement unit is a direct replacement for conventional sealed-beam unit.

HOW TO AIM HEADLAMPS

Check headlamp aim after doing any work on the headlamps, such as replacing the bulbs. Also check headlamp aim after installing new springs or shocks.

You need a wall for a test area, with a level area large enough so you can park the car 25 feet from it. To make the beam pattern easier to see, work inside a garage, or wait until evening.

You will need a tape measure, masking tape, a medium Phillips-head screwdriver, and a flashlight to see the headlamp adjuster screws.

Before you begin, fill the fuel tank and make sure all tires are correctly inflated. Remove any heavy objects from the interior that are not part of the car.

Park the car with the front bumper almost touching the test area. Have someone sit in the driver's seat to simulate normal loaded conditions. Then follow the procedure in the following photos.

Make vertical and horizontal marks. *Place two 3-foot long pieces of tape vertically on the wall, about a foot off the ground and directly in line with the center of each headlamp. Then, cross the vertical strips with 2-foot long pieces of tape at the exact height of the center of the headlamps.*

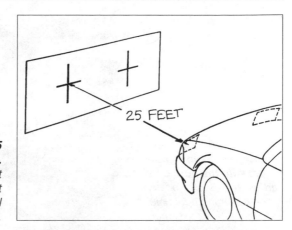

Move the car back 25 feet away from the wall. *Drive the car straight back, keeping the front bumper parallel to the wall.*

Turn the headlamps on high beam and check the beam pattern. *The high beams should be centered on the crossed tapes. If they aren't, the headlamps require aiming.*

Raise or lower the beam with the vertical adjuster—*usually located either on top of or directly below the lamp assembly.*

*Move the beam right or
left with the horizontal
adjuster—usually located
on either the right or left
side of the lamp assembly.*

PRO TIP: Special Adjustment for Trailer Towing

Before towing a trailer for long distances at night, you should check
and adjust the aim of your headlamps *with the trailer attached.*
Connect your trailer to the car or truck, fully loaded just as it will be
towed. Then adjust the beams as described on the preceding two
pages. Remember to readjust the beams back to normal when
you're finished towing the trailer.

NORMAL BEAM
ADJUSTED BEAM

**With the trailer connected, the beam will be
several degrees higher than normal.** *At a
distance of just a few hundred feet the beam can
"blind" approaching drivers.*

HOW TO REPLACE EXTERIOR AND INTERIOR LAMP BULBS

Exterior and interior lamp assemblies differ as much as car models. Examples of the more common types are shown to help you get at burned out bulbs. Also, check your Owner's Manual; some manufacturers include lamp and lens removal instructions.

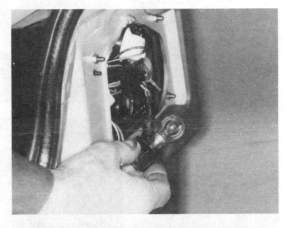

Many rear combination lamps are reached from inside the car. The twist-lock socket is almost an industry standard. Turn it counterclockwise a quarter turn to unlock it; clockwise to lock it back in place.

Large bulbs like this stop/tail lamp unit are also held in place with a twist lock.

Inspect and clean lamp sockets before installing new bulbs. *Corrosion and moisture are major causes of bulb failure. Spray WD-40 into the socket, and wipe it clean with a rag. If corrosion is severe, clean the socket with fine sandpaper— 240 to 400 grit—or emery cloth.*

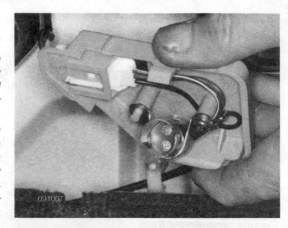

On dual-filament bulbs line up the pins on the bulb base with the slots in the socket. *One pin is lower on the base and must fit into the longer slot in the socket.*

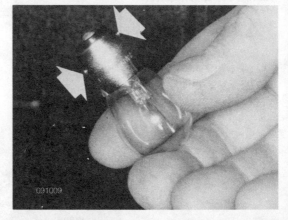

Flush-mounted lamp assemblies without visible screws are usually retained behind the panel. *Look first for a removable socket. If the lamp doesn't have one, it could be held in place with spring clips.*

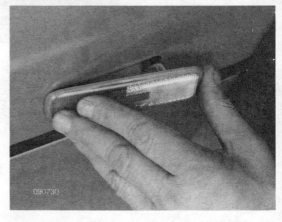

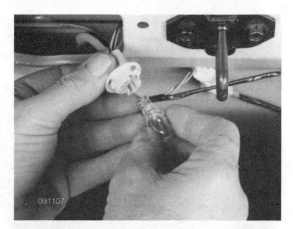

Bayonet bulbs simply push straight into their sockets. Before installing a new bulb, be sure to clean the socket with WD-40 to remove corrosion.

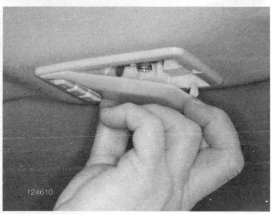

Most interior lamp lenses "snap" into place. Be extra gentle when removing this type of lens. If you must pry it loose from its base, use a small flat-blade screwdriver.

HOW TO TROUBLESHOOT BULB BURN-OUT PROBLEMS

Bulb burnout is usually caused by too high amperage, a short that causes overheating, or an intermittent that causes voltage surges. And what may seem to be bulb burnout can be filament breakage caused by vibration and physical shock from a loose socket or lamp assembly. Before you discard a bulb that isn't working, check to see if the filament is really broken or burned through. If it's in good shape, check the fuse protecting the circuit as well as all connections.

Check the socket for moisture and corrosion. The could be causing an intermittent surge that is burning out the filament. Use WD-40 and fine emery cloth to remove corrosion. Then dry it thoroughly.

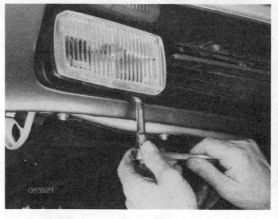

Make sure the socket and lamp assembly are securely mounted. Replace any damaged or missing vibration insulation material.

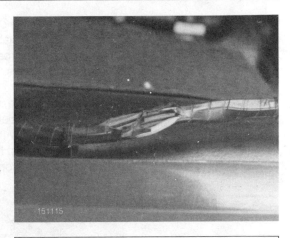

Inspect the wires for damaged insulation that could allow the wire to occasionally short out and burn out the bulb. If there is damage or burning of the wire strands, cut out the affected part and splice fresh ends together.

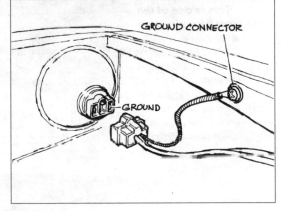

GROUND CONNECTOR

GROUND

Make sure the socket is correctly grounded. This problem is particularly common on late-model vehicles with plastic inner fenders and panels. These sockets must use a wire to the metal chassis to establish a ground circuit.

HOW TO REPAIR OR REPLACE DAMAGED WIRES

With the wide range of inexpensive electrical parts and tools available today, even unskilled beginners can do professional quality wiring repairs.

When replacing wire, always use the same gauge wire as that being replaced. And, if possible, use wire with the same color coding; you may just have to work on this part of the system sometime in the future.

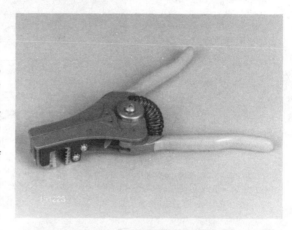

This is one of the slickest wire strippers ever made. It strips insulation neatly every time and doesn't damage the wire strands. If you're planning to do a lot of electrical work or accessory installation, this stripper is worth the few extra dollars.

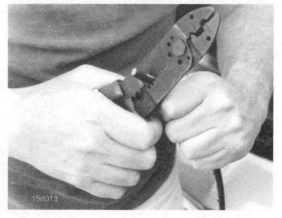

This multi-purpose wire tool cuts, strips, and crimps. It will let you make perfect crimped connections with almost no practice. However, learning to neatly strip insulation without cutting an occasional strand takes a little longer.

HOW TO REPLACE DAMAGED SOCKETS

Replacement sockets for most domestic and many imported cars and trucks are available at most auto parts stores. Hard-to-find sockets are available from dealership parts departments, although they may not be kept in stock and would have to be ordered.

As with other parts, sockets are identified by the make, model, and year in addition to the application (front turn signal, backup lamp, front sidemarker, etc.).

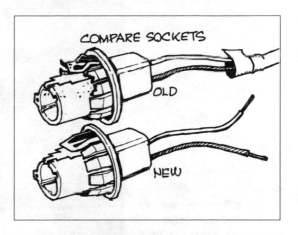

COMPARE SOCKETS

OLD

NEW

Compare the new socket with the old one to make sure it's the right one before you cut into the wiring. In multi-function sockets, such as tail/stop lamp types, compare the socket's contacts with the wires to make sure they are the same.

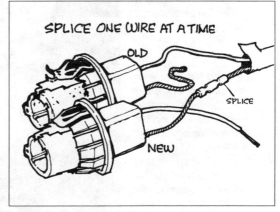

SPLICE ONE WIRE AT A TIME

OLD

NEW

SPLICE

Carefully match the wiring of the new socket to the harness. Splice one wire at a time to make sure you don't mix up circuits. If the crimping tool should break the plastic insulation on the connector, tape it with electrical tape.

PRO TIP: How to Make Perfect Splices and Connections

1. Strip 3/16-inch of insulation from the end of the wire. *Make sure you are using the correct gauge notch for the wire, or you will cut wire strands.*

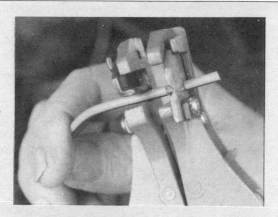

2. Slip the wire into the connector *until there is no bare wire showing.*

3. Crimp the wire with the correct crimping die. *The small pointed die is used for most automotive wiring. The large pointed die is for installing spark plug connectors on ignition wires. Use the flat die for medium and large terminal connectors.*

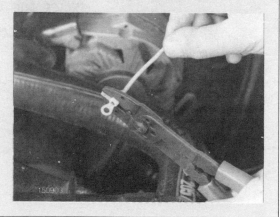

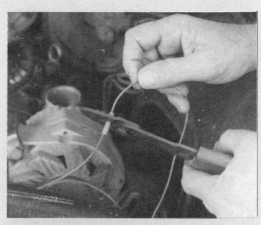

4. For splices: *insert the wires into a splice connector and crimp them in place, one at a time.*

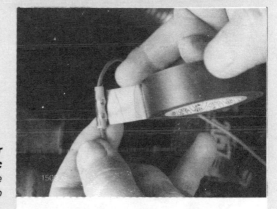

5. If the crimper breaks the plastic insulation *on the connector, tape it to prevent shorting.*

Section 11:

Fuses, Fusible Links, and Circuit Breakers

All of the electrical circuits and devices in your car or truck are protected from electrical overload and damage by fuses, fusible links, or circuit breakers.

Fuses and fusible links are designed to burn out when there is an unplanned sudden surge in electrical current, preventing damage to the wiring and accessories. Circuit breakers are used in circuits where an occasional overload is likely to occur. When this happens, the added heat causes the circuit breaker to open, "breaking" the circuit. Then, once the circuit breaker has cooled, it resets itself and restores power to the circuit. Circuit breakers do not have to be replaced unless they fail in the open position, in which case they're easy to troubleshoot because the circuit will remain "dead."

HOW TO INSPECT AND REPLACE FUSES AND FUSIBLE LINKS

Fuses protect most of the electrical circuits in your car. If an electrical component stops working, first check the fuse panel for a burned-out fuse. Many vehicles have two fuse panels—one under the hood and another under the dashboard. Also, many accessories—such as sound systems, auxiliary cooling fans, and driving lights—have individual in-line fuses between the accessory and the battery.

There are also two other types of electrical safety devices in many electrical systems: fusible links and circuit breakers. Although they can be easily replaced, you need experience to troubleshoot problems associated with these devices. If you can't restore a circuit by replacing a fuse, and you are unsure about your ability to locate and correct serious electrical problems, have the system checked by a competent specialist.

A burned-out fuse is a sign that a problem has occurred in that part of the car's electrical system protected by the fuse. It's okay to replace a fuse *once*, but if it burns out a second time, the whole circuit must be checked and repaired. Again, if you are unsure about your own troubleshooting ability, talk to a competent pro.

Never replace a fuse with one of a higher rating. If there is a problem in the circuit, the larger fuse may not burn through before the wiring and components are damaged.

Many cars have two major groups of fuses— interior and underhood. The panel for the interior fuse group—which protects most of the lighting and small accessories circuits—is usually located under the dashboard, most often at the left end.

Underhood fuse panels can be located just about anywhere in the engine compartment. If you have trouble locating one for your vehicle, check your owner's manual. These panels typically contain separate fuses for headlamp circuits, plus fusible links for ouch things as the ignition circuit, radiator cooling fans, etc.

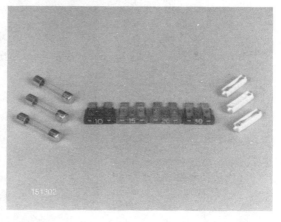

Buy an assortment of fuses and carry them in your car NOW before you need them. A couple each of 10-amp, 15-amp, 20-amp, and 30-amp fuses will handle almost all situations. Make sure you get the correct physical size and type—tube, spade, or external element.

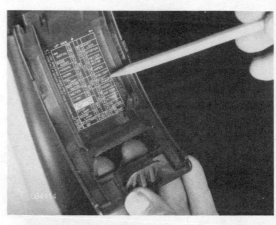

Locate the fuse for the affected system. *Check either the location sticker on the inside of the cover for the fuse block or the block itself.*

If the metal bridge is broken, the fuse is burned out. *If the bridge isn't damaged, the fuse may be good. But check it with an ohmmeter before you reinstall it. Then check connections and the wires in the circuit.*

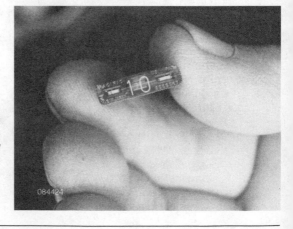

Fuses are rated by the maximum current—in amperes—they will carry. *This ampere rating appears on the fuse as well as on the location diagram.*

Fuses, Fusible Links, and Circuit Breakers

Panel-mounted fusible links are replaced the same way as fuses. However, a burned-out fusible link is an indication that there may be some serious problems in the circuit it protects, so check carefully for the cause. Correct any problem before replacing the link.

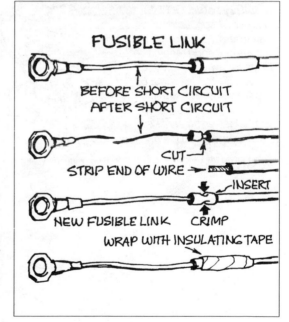

FUSIBLE LINK

BEFORE SHORT CIRCUIT
AFTER SHORT CIRCUIT

CUT
STRIP END OF WIRE

INSERT

NEW FUSIBLE LINK   CRIMP

WRAP WITH INSULATING TAPE

In-line fusible links must be spliced into the circuit they protect. Like the failure of a panel-mounted fusible link, burn out of this type signals trouble that should be found and corrected before replacing the link.

HOW TO INSTALL AN IN-LINE FUSE HOLDER

If you add any electrical accessory, such as fog lights or a stereo amplifier, be sure to install an in-line fuse as circuit protection for the safety of both the accessory and the vehicle. Electrical fires often involve most of the electrical system if not the entire vehicle.

Connect an in-line fuse holder to an un-used "pigtail" on the positive battery cable. Or make up a short connector with a large-eye terminal end and a short length of 14-gauge wire. Locate the fuse holder about 6 inches from the terminal end and tape or tie-wrap the holder to the cable so the wires won't chafe.

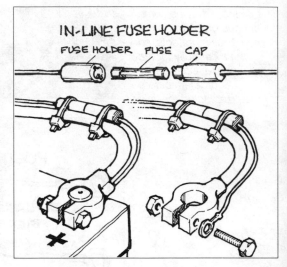

IN-LINE FUSE HOLDER

FUSE HOLDER   FUSE   CAP

Section 12:

Charging System

In this section, you will learn how to troubleshoot, test, and correct problems in the typical alternator and charging system of most vehicles on the road today. While it's not possible to cover every system ever made in a single book, you will probably find your system or a nearly identical one covered.

The charging system in your car or truck has three main components:

1. An alternator, which produces electricity.

2. A voltage regulator, which regulates the voltage going to the battery.

3. A battery, which stores electrical energy for starting, and serves as a reserve in times of high electrical use.

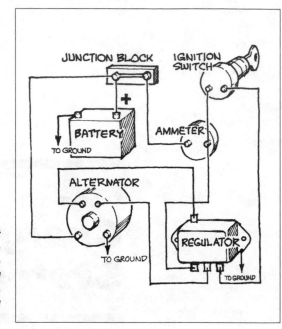

This is the component arrangement for a typical charging system with an external regulator, where the regulator is located outside the alternator.

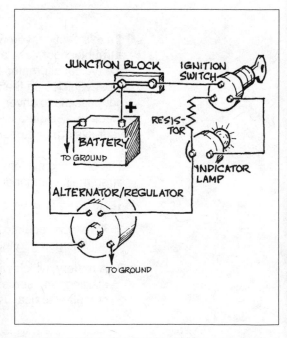

This is the component arrangement for a typical charging system with an internal regulator, where the regulator is located inside the alternator.

In most cases, the alternator produces more electricity than your car or truck can use. The surplus is used to keep the battery fully charged.

However, certain conditions can disrupt this cozy little arrangement. A fault in the alternator or regulator, a slipping alternator drive belt, or even a thin layer of corrosion between the battery cables and posts can prevent the battery from being charged.

Periods of heavy accessory use may draw electricity from the battery faster than it can be replaced, and the result will be a discharged battery.

When current draw from the battery is greater than what the alternator is supplying, a warning light on the instrument panel will glow, or the voltmeter or ammeter will indicate discharge. When the charging system is operating correctly, an ammeter will indicate a charge or "+," or a voltmeter will indicate 13 to 15 volts. Or, if your vehicle has only a warning light, the light will be out.

HOW TO TROUBLESHOOT PROBLEMS IN THE ALTERNATOR AND CHARGING SYSTEM

Charging system troubles can come from problems in the battery, the alternator, the alternator drive belt, or the voltage regulator. For this reason, it's necessary to systematically troubleshoot the charging system to pinpoint the problem. Otherwise, you may wind up replacing good parts before you find the bad one.

To use the *Quick-Check Troubleshooting Guide* on the following two pages, first find the trouble you are experiencing. This is located in the first column, *Symptom.* The symptoms described are typical and the most common ones you're likely to experience. The next column, *Possible Causes,* tells you what may be causing the problem. The last column, *Test and Remedies,* tells you how to verify and fix the problem.

To use this *Troubleshooting Guide,* hook up a voltmeter as shown below.

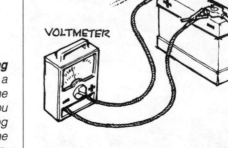

To perform charging system tests, *connect a voltmeter across the battery terminals. If you are using an analog meter, select the 30-volt DC scale.*

Battery service and testing procedures are covered on pages 97 through 103. Alternator and regulator tests begin on page 143.

Quick-Check Troubleshooting Guide: Charging System Problems

Symptom	Possible Causes	Tests and Remedies
Battery warning light comes on, and voltmeter indicates below normal.	The battery is discharging, and the alternator is not recharging it. Alternator output may be low, a defective voltage regulator could be suppressing alternator output, or poor connections may be preventing sufficient electricity from reaching the battery.	Check for a slipping alternator drive belt. Check for loose or corroded connections on the battery and alternator. Test the alternator and regulator (see pages 143-147).
Battery warning light comes on, and voltmeter indicates normal.	The battery is discharging, even though the alternator is operating. Either the alternator output is not reaching the battery because of a poor connection, or a short circuit is drawing more current from the battery than the alternator can supply.	Clean the battery terminals (page 100). Have a technician test the battery output under load and check the electrical system for unusually high current draw.
Battery warning light goes on and off, and voltmeter rises and falls.	This is usually caused by an intermittent fault in the charging system.	Check for loose connections at the battery and alternator. Loosen the drive belt and test the alternator shaft for wobble. Worn bearings could cause poor brush contact inside the alternator.
Battery warning light goes on and off, and voltmeter indicates normal.	This is usually caused by an intermittent short circuit that is drawing large amounts of power from the battery.	Test the battery for internal shorting (page 95). Have a technician check the electrical system for grounded wires or internally shorted accessories.

Electrical Service

Quick-Check Troubleshooting Continued:
Charging System Problems

Symptom	Possible Causes	Tests and Remedies
Voltmeter continuously indicating below normal.	The battery is being undercharged, either because of low alternator output, or a faulty voltage regulator.	Check alternator drive belt tension and condition. Check alternator output and regulator function (pages 143-147).
Voltmeter continuously indicating above normal.	The alternator is overcharging, due to a faulty voltage regulator. Prolonged overcharging will shorten battery life.	Check alternator output and regulator function (pages 143-147). Test the battery to see if it has been damaged by overcharging (page 102).
Battery requires frequent addition of water or lamps require frequent replacement.	The charging system is overcharging severely.	Check alternator output and regulator function (pages 143-147). Test the battery to see if it has been damaged by the overcharging (page 102).
Alternator is noisy.	Noise from the alternator could be caused by a slipping drive belt, loose mounting bolts, or wear or damage within the alternator itself.	Test the drive belt tension, and inspect the contact faces of alternator pulley and belt for glazing. Check the alternator mounting bolts for tightness. Loosen the drive belt and wiggle the alternator shaft. Any movement indicates worn bearings.

HOW TO TEST ALTERNATORS WITH EXTERNAL REGULATORS

The voltage regulator in an alternator system is located either outside of the alternator as a separate component (*external* regulator), or inside the alternator itself (*internal* regulator). These next four pages show you how to test the external regulator and three major types of external-regulator alternators from GM, Chrysler, and Ford. Page 147 shows you how to test alternators with internal regulators. Study the alternator in your car or truck and compare it with the illustrations here to tell which type you have.

Before performing any alternator/regulator tests, make sure the battery is fully charged, the connections are clean and tight, and the alternator drive belt is correctly adjusted.

Also, when testing the alternator with the regulator disconnected or disabled, test no longer than is necessary to get a voltmeter reading. Unregulated operation for more than a few seconds could damage an otherwise good alternator.

To test an external regulator: connect the positive voltmeter wire to the alternator BAT terminal, and the negative wire to ground. Connect a tach/dwell meter to the engine (see page 58). Run the engine at 1500 rpm. If the reading is 14 volts or higher, the regulator is OK. If the reading is only battery voltage, and the alternator is OK, the regulator is bad.

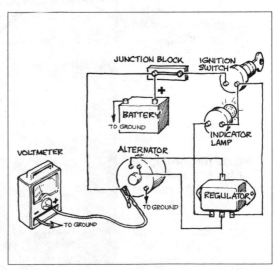

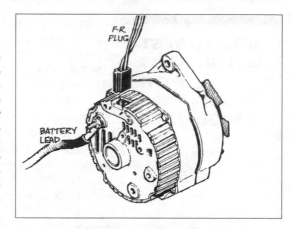

GM Delco-Remy type. The BAT terminal carries charging current to the battery with a heavy-gauge wire. The "F" wire in the plug carries current from the battery to excite the alternator "field" which enables the alternator to generate electricity. The "R" wire connects the relay functions in the regulator to the alternator.

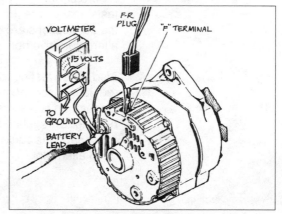

Disconnect the F-R plug and connect a jumper wire between the F terminal and the BAT terminal. Connection to the BAT terminal may produce a spark. Connect the plus wire from a voltmeter to the BAT terminal and connect the negative wire from the meter to ground.

Start and run the engine at fast idle and check the output. If the reading is 15 volts or higher, the alternator is OK. If the meter reads only battery voltage, the alternator is bad.

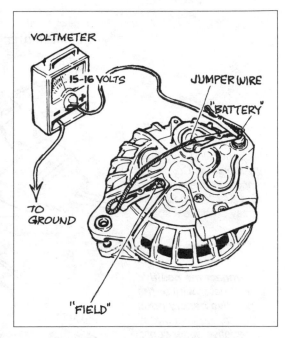

Chrysler single-field alternator. Connect a jumper wire between the field and BAT terminals. This may produce a spark. Connect the positive voltmeter wire to the BAT terminal, and the negative wire to ground. Run the engine at fast idle. If the reading is 15 volts or higher, the alternator is OK. If the meter reads only battery voltage, the alternator is bad.

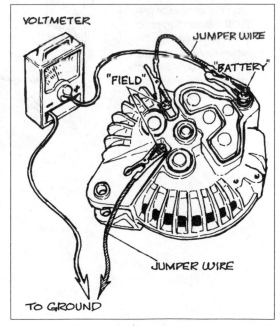

Chrysler double-field alternator. Connect a jumper wire between one field terminal and the BAT terminal. This may produce a spark. Ground the other field terminal. Connect the positive voltmeter wire to the BAT terminal, and the negative wire to ground. Run the engine at fast idle. If the reading is 15 volts or higher, the alternator is OK. If the meter reads only battery voltage, the alternator is bad.

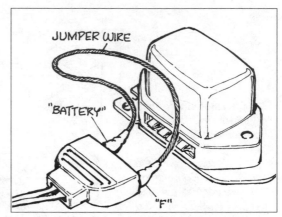

Ford externally regulated alternators. *Disconnect the plug from the regulator. Connect a jumper between the plug F and BAT terminals. This may produce a spark.*

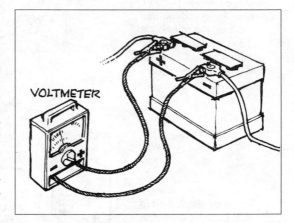

Connect the positive voltmeter wire to the positive battery post, *and the negative wire to the negative battery post. Run the engine at fast idle. If the reading is 15 volts or higher, the alternator is OK. If the meter reads only battery voltage, the alternator is bad.*

HOW TO TEST ALTERNATORS WITH INTERNAL REGULATORS

Testing an alternator with an internal regulator requires little more than hookup of the voltmeter. Before performing the test, make sure the battery is fully charged, the connections are clean and tight, and the alternator drive belt is correctly adjusted.

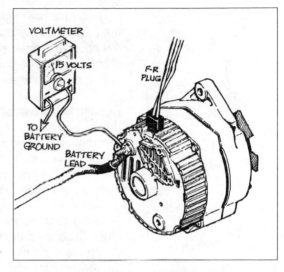

Connect the positive side of the voltmeter to the positive battery terminal, *and connect the negative side of the meter to the negative battery terminal. Start and run the engine at fast idle. If the reading is 15 volts or higher, the alternator is OK.*

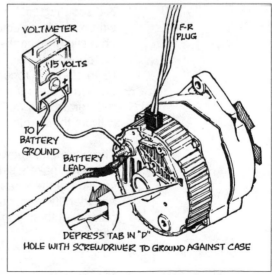

If the reading is less than 15 volts, *press in on the tab in the D hole in the rear of the alternator to bypass the regulator. If the reading is still low the alternator is defective. But, if the reading is now 15 volts or higher, the alternator is OK but the regulator is bad. In either case, replace the alternator.*

HOW TO REPLACE THE ALTERNATOR

Before we talk about *how* to replace the alternator, let's look at *why*. Obviously you wouldn't be considering buying a new alternator if you weren't having charging system trouble. But before you jump to conclusions, check the drive belt to make sure it isn't slipping. Make sure all alternator connections are clean and tight. Make sure the battery is fully charged. Finally, check out the alternator against the troubleshooting procedure that begins on page 141. Then, if you're sure the alternator is faulty, replace it.

Rebuild kits are available for alternators, but unless you have successfully rebuilt one, we recommend that you choose either a new or rebuilt replacement alternator. They cost little more than the price of the rebuild kit, plus they're guaranteed. *Your* rebuilding work isn't.

Before you start replacing your alternator, you must disconnect the battery. If you have an electronic radio with preset station memory, the memory may be erased when the battery is disconnected. Thus, it's a good idea to write your preselected radio station numbers on a slip of paper before you disconnect the battery so you can easily reprogram your radio after you reconnect it. And if you have an owner-programmable alarm, remember to reprogram it as well, or your vehicle will be without theft protection.

The alternator shown is *typical.* If yours is different, make a simple diagram of the location of the wires. Then, label the wires and identify them on your diagram so you can reconnect them correctly to your new alternator.

Unplug the connector, and disconnect the wires from the rear of the alternator. *Unscrew the nuts that attach the wires, and pull the wires off their studs.*

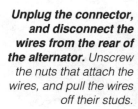

Loosen the alternator belt tensioner bolt and the pivot bolt. *Push the alternator toward the engine to remove the belt.*

Remove the tensioner and pivot bolts. *Then remove the alternator from the engine.*

Install the new alternator by reversing the removal steps. Adjust the belt tension before tightening the bolts. Belt tension is correct when you can deflect the belt 1/4 to 1/2 inch midway between the pulleys. Tighten the tension bolt first to hold the alternator in position while you tighten the pivot bolt.

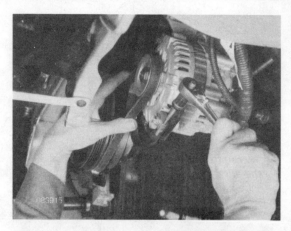

Plug in the connector, and attach the wires. Alternators with individual wires have different size terminals that fit on different size posts. So if a terminal won't fit over one post, install it on the other.

Check the operation of the new alternator. Connect the battery, start the engine, and watch the alternator light or meter. The light should go out (or the meter should indicate charge) when the engine starts. If the light stays on, shut off the engine. Recheck to make sure the wires are correctly connected and the belt is correctly adjusted.

Section 13:

Starting System

The starting system in your car or truck gets a real workout every time it's called on to start the engine. It has to be powerful and tough enough to instantly overcome the

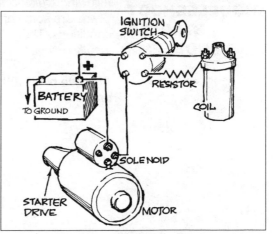

A typical starting system consists of a battery, electrical cables, a solenoid for moving the starter drive in and out of engagement with the flywheel, a drive gear to turn the ring gear on the engine, and a motor to power the drive gear.

inertia of the crankshaft and pistons and move all this dead mass with enough speed to make the engine think it's already running. Otherwise it won't start.

For the starting system to do its job all these elements must be working correctly. The battery supplying the electrical power must be fully charged. All connections must be clean and tight to ensure that enough electricity gets to where it's needed. The solenoid must be working perfectly to provide electrical power to the motor at the same time it's yanking the starter drive into engagement with the engine flywheel. And the starter motor must be strong enough to spin the engine fast enough to start it.

All you have to do is make sure that all of the components in the starting system are in good working order.

HOW TO TROUBLESHOOT STARTER PROBLEMS

Problems with the starting system are fairly easy to identify. The symptoms shown on the following *Quick-Check Troubleshooting Guide* are some of the more common conditions. They all assume that the battery is *fully charged*.

Also see page 158 for more general starting problems.

Quick-Check Troubleshooting Guide: Starter Problems

Symptom	Possible Causes	Tests and Remedies
Starter turns slowly or not at all.	If the starter turns too slowly to start the engine, or just produces a clicking sound, it is not receiving enough electricity.	To see if the battery cable connections are good, turn on the headlights as you crank the starter. If the lights dim, clean the battery terminals and posts. Try the starter again with the lights on.
		If the lights dim dramatically when you turn the key, the starter is probably shorted to ground and should be replaced (page 155).
		If the lights stay bright when you turn the key, the problem could be either a faulty ignition switch or solenoid. Have the starting system tested by a technician.
Starter turns but does not disengage when you release the key.	If the starter continues to turn after the engine is running, the pinion gear is still meshed with the ring gear. This is usually caused by a sticking solenoid or shift fork.	Check the starter to make sure it has not come loose. If necessary, retighten the mounting bolts (page 156). If the starter is firmly in place, remove it to see whether the pinion gear is stuck in its extended position, and inspect the condition of the gear teeth.
	A fault in the ignition switch may keep the solenoid energized after you've released the key.	If the pinion gear is retracted and the teeth are okay, have the ignition switch tested.
	It is possible that the pinion gear is jamming in the ring gear because the starter is loose, or the gear teeth are rough.	

Quick-Check Troubleshooting Continued: Starter Problems

Symptom	Possible Causes	Tests and Remedies
Starter spins but the engine does not turn.	A high-speed whirring sound indicates that the starter motor is working, but something is preventing the pinion drive gear on the starter from engaging with the driven ring gear on the engine flywheel. There are several possible problems:

The starter may be loose and cocked, so the pinion gear cannot contact the ring gear.

The starter solenoid or shift fork may be sticking, preventing the pinion gear from moving into place.

The ring gear may be missing teeth at the point opposite the starter, giving the pinion gear nothing to engage with. | Check to see that the starter is firmly in place. If loose, tighten it.

Remove the starter and check the pinion gear teeth on it. If they are worn or damaged, replace the starter (facing page). If the starter pinion gear teeth are damaged, there is a good possibility the flywheel ring gear will also be bad.

Look into the starter opening and inspect the flywheel ring gear. (This may require a flashlight and a mirror.) If the ring gear is damaged, have the flywheel replaced by a technician.

If the pinion and ring gears are okay, the starter solenoid or the shift fork are defective and should be replaced. |
| Starter makes grinding noises. | A grinding noise usually indicates that the pinion and ring gears aren't meshing properly. It can also be caused by worn components in the starter motor itself. | Check to see that the starter is firmly in place. If loose, tighten it.

Remove the starter and inspect the gear teeth for damage and wear. If the teeth are in good condition, have the starter bench-tested. |

HOW TO REPLACE THE STARTER

A starter will usually give you some warning when it's about to fail. It may be balky, or noisy, or it may not always engage completely. However, before you blame the starter, make sure the battery is fully charged and its terminals are clean and tight. And double-check the symptoms against those shown in the *Quick-Check Troubleshooting Chart* on the preceding two pages.

This is a simple job. However, you'll be lying on your back, looking up, so protect your eyes from falling dirt with either clear goggles or safety glasses.

Before you begin, disconnect the battery. Safely raise and support either the front or rear of the vehicle securely on jack stands, depending on whether the engine is in the front or the rear.

WARNING: Never get under a vehicle supported only by a jack. Use automotive jack stands or ramps to safely secure the vehicle.

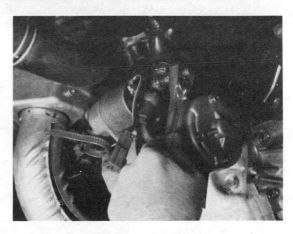

Disconnect the small wire and the large positive cable from the solenoid. Make a mental note of how they are connected so you can reinstall them correctly on the new starter.

Electrical Service

Support the starter as you remove the mounting bolts. Loosen both bolts first, and unscrew them progressively so they support the weight of the starter. Finally, pull the bolts, and remove the old starter.

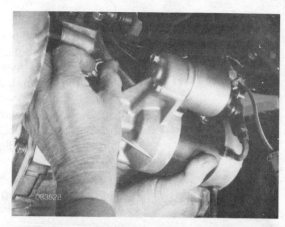

Inspect the starter pinion gear and the flywheel ring gear. If there is wear or damage on one, there is likely to be wear or damage on the other. This gear is in good condition.

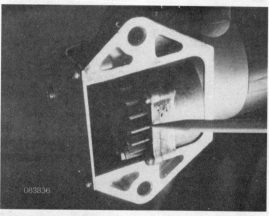

Install the new starter by reversing the removal steps. First install one bolt part way to support the starter. Then install the other bolt, and tighten them both to about 40 ft-lb (54 N.m).

Connect the cable to the large threaded post on the solenoid, and screw on the nut. *Be careful when tightening the nut not to damage the solenoid. Then connect the solenoid wire.*

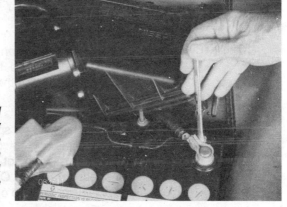

Lower the car, and connect the battery cables. *Connect the positive cable first, then the negative. Check out your new starter to make sure it works properly.*

HOW TO TROUBLESHOOT GENERAL STARTING PROBLEMS

Not all starting problems are starter problems. Most starting and running problems can be traced to faults in the ignition system, with the remainder being made up of fuel supply problems and actual mechanical failures.

There are several simple troubleshooting tasks you can do to identify the general nature of problems in the ignition or fuel systems. This will help you determine if you can repair it yourself or should refer the job to an expert. Also see the *Quick-Check Troubleshooting Guide* on page 153 for problems specifically related to the starter itself.

Check for spark. Check out the ignition system, starting with the spark plug wires, to determine if high voltage is reaching the spark plugs.

WARNING: Before checking for spark, check for gas fumes in the engine compartment. If you can smell gas, do not arc the spark plugs or spark plug wires. Otherwise an explosion is likely to occur.

Spark from the ignition coil is extremely high voltage and can cause severe injury. Use a glove or a dry cloth to insulate your hand.

Disconnect one of the spark plug wires, and hold the boot about a 1/4 inch above its plug. Have an assistant crank the engine for several seconds. If you hear a sharp "snap" or see a fat blue spark, the ignition system is in good shape and the problem is likely in the fuel system.

If you get a weak yellow spark, or none at all, test the remaining plug wires for spark, one at a time. If only one or two wires are developing poor sparks, inspect the wires and their connections. If you have an ohmmeter, measure the wire resistance (see page 46) and replace any wire that has more than 30,000 ohms resistance.

If only one or two wires are developing a poor spark, inspect the appropriate terminals inside the distributor cap (see page 53).

If you do not get a spark at any plug, work backward through the ignition system to see where the fault lies.

Disconnect the coil wire from the distributor cap, and hold it 1/4 inch from its terminal or a ground, and repeat the spark test. If the spark is strong, the trouble is in the distributor cap or rotor.

If there is no spark, inspect the coil wire for damage, and check the coil connector plug for looseness and corrosion.

If you still don't get a spark, there is a fault elsewhere in the ignition system that should be diagnosed by a competent pro.

Check for fuel and fuel flow.

1. Check the fuel gauge and the tank for sufficient fuel. This seems obvious, but tow truck operators will tell you that the majority of their "won't start" calls are because the vehicle is out of gas.

2. On carbureted engines: remove the air cleaner and operate the throttle to see if the accelerator pump is squirting gas into the carburetor. If you know there is gas in the tank but none is squirted into the carburetor, you may have a clogged filter or a bad fuel pump.

3. On carbureted engines: disconnect the fuel line from the fuel pump at the fuel filter and place a metal can under it. Have someone crank the engine for a couple of revolutions while you check for gas flow.

WARNING: Be careful to catch gasoline in a metal container and keep it away from the engine. Gasoline is a major fire hazard, so no smoking, open flames, or sparks.

If you see gas flow from the fuel line: The filter is probably clogged and should be replaced.

If you see no gas flow: The fuel pump is probably not working.

Be sure to reconnect the fuel line.

NOTE: This list of engine firing order is supplied to assist you with solid lifter valve adjustment. *CAUTION:* Always check the exact firing order of *your* engine. It is generally stamped or cast on the engine's intake manifold, valve cover, or cylinder head.

V8 Engines
American Motors, all: 1-8-4-3-6-5-7-2
Buick, all: 1-8-4-3-6-5-7-2
Cadillac 350: 1-8-4-3-6-5-7-2
Chevy, all: 1-8-4-3-6-5-7-2
Chrysler, all: 1-8-4-3-6-5-7-2
International, all: 1-8-4-3-6-5-7-2
Jeep, all: 1-8-4-3-6-5-7-2
Oldsmobile, all: 1-8-4-3-6-5-7-2
Pontiac, all: 1-8-4-3-6-5-7-2
Cadillac 472, 500: 1-5-6-3-4-2-7-8
Ford Small V8 (C & W): 1-3-7-2-6-5-4-8
Ford, Mercury, Lincoln Big V8: 1-5-4-2-6-3-7-8

V6 Engines
Chevy: 1-6-5-4-3-2
Buick: 1-6-5-4-3-2
Olds: 1-6-5-4-3-2
Pontiac: 1-6-5-4-3-2
Ford/Mercury, all: 1-4-2-5-3-6
Jeep: 1-2-3-4-5-6
Chrysler: 1-2-3-4-5-6
Dodge: 1-2-3-4-5-6
Plymouth: 1-2-3-4-5-6

In-Line 6 Engines
American Motors: 1-5-3-6-2-4
Chevy, Buick, Olds, &
Pontiac (includes OHC): 1-5-3-6-2-4
Chrysler, Dodge, &
Plymouth Slant 6: 1-5-3-6-2-4
Ford, all: 1-5-3-6-2-4
Jeep: 1-5-3-6-2-4
Toyota: 1-5-3-6-2-4

Opposed 6 Engines
Chevy Corvair: 1-4-5-2-3-6
Porsche: 1-6-2-4-3-5

In-Line 4 Engines
Chevy, Olds, Pontiac all: 1-3-4-2
Ford Pinto Big 4: 1-3-4-2
Dodge/Plymouth: 1-3-4-2
Datsun/Nissan: 1-3-4-2
Honda: 1-3-4-2
International: 1-3-4-2
Isuzu/LUV: 1-3-4-2
Jeep: 1-3-4-2
Mazda/Courier: 1-3-4-2
Mitsubishi: 1-3-4-2
Opel: 1-3-4-2
Toyota, 20R, 22R, 22RE: 1-3-4-2
VW: 1-3-4-2
Ford Pinto Small 4: 1-2-4-3
Toyota 3Y-EC: 1-2-4-3

Opposed 4 Engines
VW/Porsche Flat 4: 1-4-3-2
Subaru: 1-4-3-2

**APPENDIX B:
COMPRESSION
RECORD**

Use this page to keep a record of the compression readings of your vehicle's engine during the period of ownership. See page 29 for a full explanation of compression testing.

Date	Cylinder Compression, psi							
	1	2	3	4	5	6	7	8

Date	Cylinder Compression, psi							
	1	2	3	4	5	6	7	8

APPENDIX C: VEHICLE SERVICE DATA

Make_____Model __ ____Year _____

VIN_____

Engine_____Trans. _____

Color code _____ Trim code _____

Spark plug type _____ Gap _____

Point gap _____ Dwell angle _____

Ignition timing _____

Idle speed _____

Oil cap. _____ Grade _____

Trans. cap._____ Grade _____

Diff. cap. _____ Grade _____

4WD:

  T-case cap. _____ Grade _____

  Front axle cap._____ Grade _____

Coolant cap. _____

Fuel cap. _____

Air filter Part No. _____

PCV valve Part No. _____

Fuel filter Part No. _____

Battery No._____ Rating_____

Alternator belt Part No. _____

Power steering belt Part No. _____

AIR pump belt Part No. _____

AC compressor belt No. _____

Water pump belt Part No. _____

Tire size_____

Air pressure: Front_____ __Rear _____

VEHICLE SERVICE DATA

Make_____Model _____Year_____

VIN _____

Engine_____Trans._____

Color code_____ Trim code _____

Spark plug type_____Gap _____

Point gap_____ Dwell angle_____

Ignition timing _____

Idle speed _____

Oil cap. _____ Grade _____

Trans. cap. _____ Grade _____

Diff. cap. _____ Grade _____

4WD:
  T-case cap. _____Grade _____

  Front axle cap. _____Grade _____

Coolant cap. _____

Fuel cap. _____

Air filter Part No. _____

PCV valve Part No._____

Fuel filter Part No._____

Battery No. _____Rating _____

Alternator belt Part No. _____

Power steering belt Part No. _____

AIR pump belt Part No._____

AC compressor belt No. _____

Water pump belt Part No. _____

Tire size _____

Air pressure: Front _____Rear_____

INDEX

A

Adjustment of carburetor, see Carburetor

Adjustment of valve clearance, see Mechanical lifters

Aiming headlights, see Headlights

Air filter

Correct orientation 78

Replacement on carbureted engines 77

Replacement on fuel-injected engines 78, 7

Alarm, need to reset after electrical service 97, 101, 104, 148

Alternator

Replacement 148-150

Testing external-regulator type 143-146

Testing internal-regulator type 147

see also Charging system

Aluminum cylinder heads, Pro Tip on removing spark plugs from 23

Analog volt/ohmmeter, see Volt/ohmmeter

Anti-seize compound 13, 43

B

Baking soda 89, 99

Battery cable

Cleaning terminals 100-101

Replacement 110-111

Battery

Maintenance-free service needs 97

Charging procedure 108-109

Cleaning 99-101, 105

Cold cranking amp rating 112

Dead 95-96

Deep cycle 112

Electrolyte refilling 96, 98, 101

Hold-down clamps 104-105

Internal construction 94

Key for long life 96

Never allow to discharge 96

Operation described 95

Post cleaning tool 88, 99-101

Pro Tip on basic battery specifications 112

Pro Tip on hydrometer test of charge 102-103

Pro Tip on selecting correct replacement 106-107

Replacement 104-105

Reserve capacity rating 112

Safety warnings 98

Servicing procedure 97-103

Specific gravity chart 103

Test for internal shorting 95

Test with hydrometer for charge 102-103

Types available 106-107

see also Charging system

see also Starting system

BMW test for gasoline cleaning additives 70
Brake light bulbs, see Light bulbs
Breaker cam grease 14, 55
BTDC, see Ignition timing
Bulbs, see Light bulbs

C

Cables, see Ignition cables
Carbon tracks 53
Carburetor
  Cleaning 68-69, 13
  Correct sequence for tune-up 5
  Fast-idle speed adjustment 81-82
  Idle speed adjustment 79-80, 81
  Mixture adjustment 81-82
  see also Air filter, Fuel filter, and Fuel system troubleshooting
Centrifugal advance, see Distributor
Charging system
  Alternator replacement 148-150
  Description 137-139
  Normal ammeter or voltmeter readings 139
  Testing alternator with external regulator 143-146
  Testing alternator with internal regulator 147
  Troubleshooting procedure 140-147
Chrysler
  Alternator testing 145
  Typical hook-up of remote starter switch 35

Circuit breakers, see Fuses
Clattering hydraulic lifters, see Hydraulic lifters
Cleaning, see specific component
Coil
  Primary wire 57
  Pro Tip on correct polarity hook up 61
  Pro Tip on disconnecting to prevent engine starting 75
Cold cranking amp rating of battery 112
Colder spark plug range, see Spark plugs
Compression gauge 14, 31
Compression test
  Correct sequence in tune-up 5
  Dry 30, 31
  High-tech engine 6
  Interpreting results 33
  Log Appendix B
  Performing 32
  Pro Tip on how to connect remote starter switch 34-35
  Purpose of 29
  Wet 30, 31
Condenser, see Distributor
Contact points, see Distributor
Crankshaft, turning for valve adjustment 22, 27
Cylinder compression, see Compression test

D

E

F

G

LUBRICATION CONTENTS: 1 Save Money with Frequent Maintenance: • Why more frequent maintenance costs less • How to keep you vehicle under warranty with DIY work **2 Parts, Supplies, and Tools:** • The rundown on what you need **3 Engine Oil and Filter Change:** • How to select the best oil and additives • Is synthetic oil right for your engine? • How to read oil condition • How to change oil and filter correctly **4 Steering and Suspension:** • How to install permanent grease fittings • How to lube steering and suspension • How to inspect for bushing wear • How to replace constant-velocity (CV) joint boots • How to check springs and torsion bars **5 Transmission and Drivetrain:** • How to change manual transmission oil • How to interpret fluid condition • How to change automatic transmission fluid and screen "leak-free" • How to inspect and change differential oil • How to lube driveshaft slip joints • How to service front wheel bearings **6 Four-Wheel Drive:** • How to change differential oil • How to change transfer case oil • How to lube slip joints and front-axle CV-joints

CHASSIS MAINTENANCE CONTENTS: 7 Drive Belts: • How to inspect and adjust • How to select the correct type • How to replace • How to put together a "free" emergency belt kit **8 Cooling System:** • Complete cooling system "tune-up" • How to test coolant freeze-protection capability • How to install a permanent coolant flushing fitting • How to reverse-flush the cooling system • How to inspect and replace radiator and heater hoses • How to replace the thermostat **9 Brake System:** • How to check and replenish brake fluid • How to inspect disk brake pads and rotor • How to fix squealing disk brakes • How to inspect and replace brake fluid • How to bleed a brake system • How to flush and replace the fluid **10 Shock Absorbers:** • How to test shock and strut condition • How to select and replace • Understanding mountings **11 Exhaust System:** • How to inspect the complete exhaust system **12 Body:** • How to lubricate body hinges and latches • How to select and replace wipers.

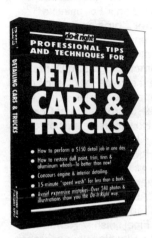

This is a book on complete appearance care—*from routine washing and waxing to show-quality preparation.*

192 pages, 300 illustrations
ISBN 1-879110-17-2

CONTENTS: 1 The Detailing Process:

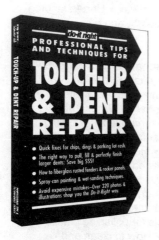

192 pages, 338 illustations
ISBN 1-879110-18-0

CONTENTS: